I would like to offer a very special thank you
to the following people:

Rev. Daisybelle Thomas-Quinney

Reverend Quinney was the first person to ever encourage me to write a book. "Son you can't allow all of these good things in your head to go to waste. Write a book, write some books."

LaTisha Hamlett Cherry

Almost five years ago my sister, LaTisha, had an idea. "Brother, have you ever thought about writing a book? I think you can do it. All of the sermons and sermon series you've done over the years. That's fifty-five or sixty books right there."

Flora Bertrand

After finding out about my intentions of writing a book, my cousin Flora refused to let me not write the book. She hounded me for years, "Are you finished with the book? Cousin, come on now, where are you on that book? Okay, what about the book?"

This Book is dedicated to:

My Lord and Savior Jesus Christ
Who saved me by His grace, loved me unconditionally, and blessed me beyond measure. He truly makes all things possible.

Candace
My loving wife, who is my biggest fan, and my very best friend. Her love for me has never failed. She is the half of me that is the best part of me.

Henry and Louella Cherry
My wonderful parents gave me life and so much more. I am forever grateful for their support, love, and confidence in me. They are worthy of triple honor.

Family, Friends, and Hightown
I am so blessed to be connected to such wonderful people. I love you all and thank God for each of you. I pray that His best will always be yours.

Contents

Introduction 7
Chapter One: Your Destination Is Divine 11
Chapter Two: Read The Map 21
Chapter Three: Fully Equipped 37
Chapter Four: Move To The Passenger Seat 49
Chapter Five: Locate The Glory 59
Chapter Six: Let's Go 71
Chapter Seven: Driven By Passion 81
Chapter Eight: Follow Peace 95
Chapter Nine: Don't Stop 107
Chapter Ten: Arrive At Your Destination 121
Prayer For Salvation 131
About The Author 132

My Purpose
HIS PLAN

Success

Road Closed

Purpose

Stop

Detour

Destiny

A ROAD MAP
TO YOUR
DESTINY AND
GOD'S WILL
FOR YOUR LIFE

Marvin D. Cherry

My Purpose His Plan

A Road Map To Your Destiny and God's Will For Your Life

ISBN-13: 978-0-692-10539-9
ISBN-10: 0-692-10539-5

DRAGON REALM PRESS

INTRODUCTION

God has created each of us for a real purpose. I believe that as children of our Heavenly Father, we all exist to touch humanity in some very special and positive way. I know that we have been called to do great things: to save lives, to live better, to have more, to give more, to bring hope to many, and to change our part of the world. Because we were fearfully and wonderfully made by the same God who created the universe, this could only mean one thing, we were born to win and designed for real success.

You may be saying or thinking, "Hey, that sounds great and wonderful but how do I get there? I don't feel special or important at all; in fact, most of the time, I can't tell if I'm coming or going. I don't have any money. I don't have much education. I don't have any real skills. In fact, outside of my children, the dog and the greeter at Wal-Mart, no one else really knows I exist." Trust me, I hear you. I hear you loud and clear. But, the good news is that you are alive! Right now you're reading this book and that means that you're breathing, and blood is running through your veins; hey, that's good news and it's a good start. YOU ARE ALIVE; therefore, there's hope for you and your future.

Everything you said about your current situation may be true and factual, but you can begin to change those facts with your faith. You may not know how to do it or even where or how to get started. That's okay because you have a sovereign God who knows all about you and your destiny and how to get you there.

There are millions of people out there who feel the same way you do. They ask some of the same questions that you ask every day. Why am I here? How do I get to where I really want to be? How can I have a better life and a more meaningful existence? As a matter of fact, what is life really all about anyway? These questions are often the source of much frustration for many people who truly love the Lord.

We often wish that God would speak with a loud voice from heaven and tell us exactly what to do and when to do it. Then there are those times when we pray that God's handwriting would somehow appear on the walls, immediately giving us our answers and instructing us on when and how to make our next move.

But it is very rare that God would give us all of the specific information and details that we need for success in our lives all at once. He does, however, invite us to draw near to Him and promises to draw near to us, revealing Himself and His will. He also allows us the freedom to make choices and decisions that are in alignment and agreement with His Word and His will.

He expects us to trust not in our own human understanding, but to acknowledge Him in all of our ways so that He may direct our paths. So, how do we come to know the mind of

God? How do we know what His will is for our lives? As we seek His face, He will begin to reveal His great purpose and plan for our lives.

As we walk in obedience and love, He will actually put His desires in our hearts. We must then embrace, trust, celebrate, and exalt Him with all that is in us. When we do this, something awesome and amazing will begin to unfold for all to see. King David talked about it in Psalm 37:4 – "Delight yourself in the LORD and He will give you the desires of your heart."

The Lord will literally cause all of your dreams to become reality because your deep love and main desire is always for Him. Jesus Christ came all the way from heaven to earth to make it possible for us to have a good life, a productive life, and a fulfilled life, right here on earth. He is not satisfied with us just having life, but it is His desire that we experience an abundant life.

> *"I came that they may have and enjoy life, and have it in abundance (to the full, till it overflows)." John 10:10 – (Amplified Bible)*

Do you believe this? Is this the kind of life that you would like to have, one that is full and overflowing? Well, you can, but not until you decide that where you would rather be is better than where you are right now. Understand that your life is the journey that will carry you to your divine destination.

As you continue to read and meditate on the contents of this book, get ready to go from where you are to where God has always wanted you to be. It's your purpose; but, it's His plan. Come on, let's get going!

CHAPTER ONE

YOUR DESTINATION IS DIVINE

Divine: Emanating or coming from God.

As you begin the journey of discovering your purpose for life, please know and understand that your destination is truly divine. That's right; your ultimate destiny is of God and it comes from God. Your great purpose was born out of the Father's love for you. So who better to seek for answers to the questions that you now have about your life than God? Scripture teaches us to look unto Jesus who is the author and finisher of our faith. The Lord wrote the book on you and it is a good book with a happy ending! You are connected to the God of this universe and all that is good comes from Him and His amazing grace and love for you.

GOD HAS A GOOD PLAN FOR YOUR LIFE

Did you know that God, your Heavenly Father, has a plan for your life? It is a good plan. It is a perfect plan designed especially for you. This plan was created before you were even born. In fact, God has seen your end and your middle even from the very beginning; and now, He is eager to show it to you. As a believer, you can claim what is written about you in the Bible.

> *Jeremiah 29:11 – For I know the thoughts that I think toward you, saith the LORD, thoughts of peace, and not of evil, to give you an expected end.*

Can you imagine that the God of this universe actually thinks about us? The Maker, Creator, and Sustainer of all things has thoughts about you. This could only mean one thing, God loves you and you're very special to Him.

Look at this verse again, "For I know the thoughts that I think toward you, saith the LORD, thoughts of peace, and not of evil, to give you an expected end." Notice that God not only thinks about us, but His thoughts about us are always good. They are always thoughts of peace and not evil. His desire for us is to have a good life with a good future. This is because we serve and belong to Him, our good God. In John's gospel, Jesus is recorded as saying this, "The thief cometh not, but for to steal, and to kill, and to destroy: I am come that they might have life, and that they might have it more abundantly." Satan's purpose is stated and it is quite clear that his mission is to harm us and to bring devastation into our lives. But, Jesus came to do just the opposite. His mission was to bring to us the hope of a good life. God is not satisfied with His people just existing or having life. He wants us to experience an abundant life, a life that is actually filled with life.

> *John 10:10b – I came that they may have and enjoy life, and have it in abundance (to the full, till it overflows). - AMP*

That's it! That is exactly what God wants for His people. He wants us to have a good quality of life.

It is His will that we enjoy our lives until it overflows. This is the good plan that He has always had in mind for us. Begin to embrace and meditate on that idea. See yourself the way He sees you and begin to think about you the way God thinks about you. Go ahead and receive His plan for your life. It's good, it's perfect, its fail-proof and it's yours!

GOD KNOWS EVERYTHING ABOUT YOU AND YOUR JOURNEY

God knows everything that there is to know about you and your destiny. He knows and understands the mess-ups, the mix-ups, the missteps, the mishaps, the mistakes, and of course, the set-backs. Nothing about you will ever take God by surprise. Remember, He sees the end of a thing in the very beginning. So then, He knows just how to get you to your ultimate destination. He knows the way because He is the way and has already gone before you.

Let's face it, God is still omniscient, meaning He knows everything, and no one could ever say that about you or me. God's omniscience means that He perfectly and eternally knows all things which can be known: past, present, and future. There is nothing that can be known that He does not already know. Hallelujah! The psalmist said…

> *Psalm 147:4-5 – "He telleth the number of the stars; he calleth them all by their names. Great is our Lord, and of great power: his understanding is infinite."*

Now, if our Heavenly Father knows the number of stars that exist and knows them all by name, then, surely, He knows us and what lies ahead for His children. His knowledge and understanding is far beyond our comprehension. This is why we must trust Him without hesitation for our future and for the rest of our lives. In the New Testament, the apostle Peter also makes it very clear that God is always fully aware of what's going on with us and what He will do.

> *Acts 15:18 – Known to God are all his works from the beginning of the world.*

It is so very important that we spend time with the One who knows everything about all things. Where should you live? Who should you marry? Which career path should you choose? These are all legitimate questions.

They are also questions that God already has the answers to. What a mighty God we serve! This is why we love Him so much. This is why we trust Him with our today and the rest of our tomorrows.

THE WAY HAS ALREADY BEEN MADE

God, in His wise providence, has already paved the way for your successful journey to your purpose and destiny. All you have to do is get on the right road and be willing to listen and obey. God knows you better than you know yourself. He knows just how you work and what you are best suited for in life. After all, He made you, remember?

The way had already been made for a young boy we read about in the Bible named Jeremiah. When Jeremiah was still a child he received some very astonishing news from the Lord.

> *Jeremiah 1:5 – "Before I formed thee in the belly I knew thee; and before thou camest forth out of the womb I sanctified thee, and I ordained thee a prophet unto the nations."*

God was literally telling Jeremiah that his destiny was carved out even before he was conceived. Jeremiah was created for a purpose and so were you. His purpose in life would be to stand as a prophet for the Lord, and so, God designed him with this in mind.

Your purpose may be to teach first graders at a local elementary school, or to be a pastor, or a truck driver, or a stay at home mom, or a police officer, or a hair stylist, or the CEO of a company. Sometimes, we find it difficult to believe that God could actually use us for anything. We look at our short comings and imperfections and decide that we could never amount to anything great or worthwhile. It's often difficult for us to see what God sees and to know what God knows. The truth is greatness is written all in your DNA code.

Jeremiah was sure that he could not go where the Lord was sending him or even do what He had called him to do. Just as we do, he offered excuses; I'm too young and I don't speak well. Someone once said, "God does not always call the qualified but He always qualifies the one He calls." God promised the young boy that He would go with Him and that He would even put his words in Jeremiah's mouth. God did just that and then made another promise to Jeremiah. "I will hasten my word to perform it." Hallelujah! All we have to do is believe what God has said about us and He will make His Word become reality in our lives.

There is no need for us to guess which way we should go or even spend a whole lot of time trying to find the right way.

Why do this when we can go straight to the source? Our Heavenly Father is that source and He knows the way because He created it.

> *Isaiah 48:17 – Thus saith the LORD, thy Redeemer, the Holy One of Israel; I am the LORD thy God which teacheth thee to profit, which leadeth thee by the way that thou shouldest go.*

Did you hear that? Our success is along the path that God Himself will lead us to. Why would He do this for us? Why would He make it this easy? It's simple; He does it because He loves us and He is our God! The Lord has already made the way; we just need to follow it by following Him.

WE CANNOT GET THERE WITHOUT HIM

A big mistake we often make is thinking we can get there without the Lord. The truth be told, most of the time we don't even know where "there" is. Would you believe it if I told you that you could not trust yourself to get where He wants you to be? Well, that's exactly what I'm saying. In fact, the person that trusts in their own understanding will make the wrong decision and go down the wrong road every time. We do not have the ability to make wise decisions on our own. We must seek God through prayer and trust Him explicitly.

King Solomon said in the book of Proverbs that, "Every way of a man is right in his own eyes: but the LORD pondereth the hearts." He also said in the same book, chapter 16 and verse 25 that, "There is a way that seemeth right unto a man, but the end thereof are the ways of death." We don't have to choose a way that seems right; we can choose the way that is right.

Our way could very well lead to our demise and this is never God's will for us.

> *Proverbs 3:5-6 -"Lean on, trust in, and be confident in the Lord with all your heart and mind and do not rely on your own insight or understanding. In all your ways know, recognize, and acknowledge Him, and He will direct and make straight and plain your paths."*
> *– AMP*

This passage further proves that we cannot trust ourselves. We cannot discover or know what's best for us through human strength and intellect, alone. We must lean on God and put all of our confidence in Him.

God wants us to choose Him and His way every time. Why? Because, His way is right every time. His way promises and produces victory and not defeat; joy and not sorrow, honor and not embarrassment; hope and not destruction; peace and not war; love and not hate. His way produces our destiny.

We must be willing to surrender our will (pride and selfish motives) to God's will. When we do this God will direct our paths which will lead us to our purpose. Let's face it, we cannot get there without Him.

CHAPTER TWO

READ THE MAP

Map: A visual representation of an area.

Although somewhat outdated, most of us have had the experience of using a road map. We use maps not only to locate places but also to get to those places. The Bible is the believer's guide and road map for a successful life here on earth. This map never has to be updated because its contents never change. All of its pages are divine and each one of them tells the story of a Father and His Son and their desire to bring us all together as a beautiful family to a wonderful place.

If we study this map, it will lead us to a life of victory filled with great meaning that only heaven can offer. There is such a place and that place is waiting for each us to arrive.

ALWAYS START WITH THE MAP (THE BIBLE)

As a young boy, I have fond memories of taking road trips with my family. Back then, the first thing my parents would do before going on a long trip was to make sure that they had a map. My father and I would study the map days in advance of our trips. The map laid out the directions, the route, possible pit stops, and all of the major cities we would travel through. Our trips always started with the map.

The successful life has a starting place as well. In fact, all things have their beginning in the Word of God.

> *Hebrews 11:3 – "And we know that worlds were framed by the Word of God."*

With this in mind, isn't it only fitting that we begin the journey to our destiny on earth with the Word of God? So many times, we start off wrong and hope to end up right. But the purposeful life does not work that way.

We often begin our life's trip in reverse because we put our trust in ourselves instead of God and His Word.
Over the years, I have personally learned that you can't get very far in this world if you're always going in reverse. Where and what we need to focus on is in front of us and not behind us.

Let's face it, the path before us may be unknown to us, but it is always known by God. The road ahead could very well be difficult, dangerous, and confusing at times. There may be detours, potholes, accidents, and some roads may even be closed. Out there on your personal highways, you may encounter situations that could result in serious injury or even death.

But still, you must travel. As Christians, we must learn to travel by faith and not by sight. Where do we get this faith that's needed for the journey ahead of us? The BIBLE!

> *Romans 10:17 – So then faith cometh by hearing, and hearing by the word of God.*

That's what I love about the Word of God, it produces faith. It develops strong faith in us so that we can believe and receive the many promises of God. How often do you hear and read the Word of God? You must understand that the level of your faith determines how far you believe you can go in life. I believe you can go all the way! Isn't that exciting? God has called you to be great and to do great things. He has called you to make a difference, to excel, and to succeed in every area of your life. And you can!

The bible is the all-time best seller and most of us have our fair share of them lying around in our homes, cars, bedrooms, and nicely displayed as center pieces on our coffee tables.

But, owning all the bibles in the world is of no value if we never read them, believe them, or obey them. The Bible could very well be the best sold book that is never read. God will provide faith for our journey, but we must be willing to open our eyes and ears to receive it. The Word of God is one of life's most powerful tools. Read it; believe it; and share the good news of it with others!

FOLLOW THE DIRECTIONS

It was my own pride and arrogance that caused me to be late for some very important appointments throughout my life, and to miss some altogether. I'm talking about not following directions properly or simply not using them at all. Yes, I've been guilty of that. Years ago, some of my co-workers and I went to a workshop in Mississippi. We decided to drive our own vehicles since it was a fairly short trip and we all would be coming back to the office at different times of the day. That day we decided to follow each other. That's when I came up with a wonderful idea. I decided to go a different way, a better way, a quicker way, my way. After being separated from the group for over forty-five minutes, I called one of my buddies to check on them. I asked, "Man where are yall?" He answered, "Together at the workshop in Meridian." I was the only one not there. Why, because I was still on my way there. I was lonely, lost, laughed at, and late because I decided to follow my own way.

Following the right directions keeps us on schedule and on target. Following the right directions also keeps us from going in circles and getting lost. We live in a world where timing is everything. The Word of God offers clear and concise directions for the person who desires a productive life that's filled with purpose and meaning.

Psalm 119:105 says, Thy word is a lamp unto my feet, and a light unto my path.

Without the Word of God, we stumble and fall, and sometimes we crash and burn. That may sound harsh, but still it's true. The Bible provides guidance and assistance to those who are in a relationship with its Author.

The Word of God literally shines the Light on the way we should go and even how and when we should go. The Word of God directs us down the paths of righteousness and to the destination the Lord has designed for us.

Psalm 119:133 - Order my steps in thy word: and let not any iniquity have dominion over me.

Following God's directions that are clearly printed in the Bible will cause us to avoid many would-be accidents and road blocks. These accidents and road blocks will keep us from moving forward. Remember, the way to our destiny, is forward.

Proverbs 6:22-23 – "When thou goest, it shall lead thee; when thou sleepest, it shall keep thee; and when thou awakest, it shall talk with thee. For the commandment is a lamp; and the law is light; and reproofs of instruction are the way of life: The "it" that Solomon is referring to is the Word of God. He speaks of it as if the Bible is a person that's alive. Actually, it is alive, because, Jesus Christ is the Word and He is alive.

John 1:1-12 – In the beginning was the Word, and the Word was with God, and the Word was God. The same was in the beginning with God. All things were made by him; and without him was not any thing made that was made. In him was life; and the life was the light of men. And the light shineth in darkness; and the darkness comprehended it not. There was a man sent from God, whose name was John. The same came for a witness, to bear witness of the Light, that all men through him might believe. He was not that Light, but was sent to bear witness of that Light. That was the true Light, which lighteth every man that cometh into the world. He was in the world, and the world was made by him, and the world knew him not. He came unto

his own, and his own received him not. But as
many as received him, to them gave he power
to become the sons of God, even to them that
believe on his name:

John is speaking of none other than Jesus Christ, the Son of the Living God. The Bible is the only book that is actually alive. You may be asking, "How can a book be alive?" The Bible literally speaks to every situation in our lives. God does not leave us alone to try and figure out His will for our lives all by ourselves, He simply tells us. He speaks to us through His mighty, and powerful word. Hebrews 4:12 says that God's Word is "living and active."

God speaks to us through the words of the Bible. As we read them, we're not reading ordinary words, but words that come directly from the mind and the mouth of The Living God. The Lord's will for our lives is imbedded in the pages of the Bible. We have the privilege of reading His inspired word and internalizing His principles, which will lead to a full, exciting, and purposeful life.

2 Timothy 3:16 – All scripture is God-
breathed and is useful for teaching, rebuking,
correcting, and training in righteousness.

The phrase God-breathed literally means, "Breathed out from God." In other words, the Bible is inspired by God and comes from God. This is what makes the Bible so different and unique from all other religious writings.

It reveals God, and His ways, grace, love, thoughts, and purpose for His people. Following God's directions will always get us to where we're supposed to be.

WATCH THE SIGNS

We all have seen the road signs that line the streets and highways. Many of those signs are warning signs: road closed, wrong way, yield, do not enter, stop, or slow down. The consequences for disobeying these warning signs can lead to serious problems, fines, accidents, and sometimes even death. Those signs are placed along the roads to keep us safe, and to keep us headed in the right direction, so that we can eventually make it to our destination.

The roads of life posts warning signs as well, and not heeding those warning signs could lead to unnecessary pain, suffering, heartaches, and breakdowns. And unfortunately ignoring the important signs in life could cause us to miss our destiny altogether. Therefore, we must be careful to always pay close attention to and obey all of the road signs of life, if we expect to reach our divine destiny.

As Christians, the first sign we should notice on the road of life is JESUS. This sign stands above all of the other signs. His sign is the main sign, and the most important sign. If we keep our eyes on this sign, we will make it to where the Father is leading us.

> *John 14:6 – Jesus saith unto him, I am the way, the truth, and the life: no man cometh unto the Father, but by me.*

We know that Jesus Christ is the way to salvation, but, we should also remember that He is the way to the blessed and abundant life promised to us in the bible. Jesus is the way that leads us to our divine destiny that was carved out even before the world began. Remember, the bible says that Jesus was in the beginning and that He was the Word. This is why we must keep our eyes on Him. He must always be in full view.

What about those other signs, those warning signs that could spell disaster if we're not watchful and careful? Different signs lead us in different directions; that's why it's so important that we have a good idea as to where we're going. Some signs will lead us to roads that are going north, others will lead us to roads that are traveling south, east, or west.

There are some roads in life that we want to avoid all together. Jesus talked about two gates that we can liken to roads in the New Testament.

> *Matthew 7:13-14 – "Enter ye in at the strait gate: for wide is the gate, and broad is the*

way, that leadeth to destruction, and many there be which go in thereat: 14 Because strait is the gate, and narrow is the way, which leadeth unto life, and few there be that find it."

Following the right signs will always lead us down the right road. Jesus makes it clear, that the right road won't be crowded at all. So, don't be surprised if you don't see many people that you're acquainted with, just keep going. The Lord said only a few people would find the right road and that's because only a few would pay attention to the warning signs, and where they are going.

There are also good signs on the highways of life and they always correspond with what's on the map. I'm always amazed at how the highway signs on my GPS map show up at the same time as I'm approaching the signs on the highway. God's Word is the same way, if it's in the book or on the map, it shows up in life. God has something to say about where we've been, where we are, and where we're going. God will speak directly to us through His Word, if we're willing to put in the time to read it. When we read the map and follow the signs, here's what we can expect:

Joshua 1:8 – This book of the law shall not depart out of thy mouth; but thou shalt meditate therein day and night, that thou mayest observe to do according to all that is written therein: for then thou shalt make thy way prosperous, and then thou shalt have good success.

The Word of God produces, promotes, activates, and facilitates godly success. So, we're challenged to read it, to speak it, to meditate on it, to observe it, to be it, and to do it. If we will stay in the Word, the Word will stay in us and take us to those great places where God wants us to be.

As a child, I remember how my father would always try and keep his gas tank on full. He would never allow it to get below three-fourths of a tank. He would preach this to my mom and her sisters and brothers. He would say, "Keep the tank full and you won't ever have to worry about running out of gas and getting stranded on the road." Well guess what, the Bible is not only spiritual food, but it is also spiritual fuel. So, I say, let's fill up and let's keep our tanks full of God's spiritual fuel. If our tanks are always full, we will be able to continue driving through all the challenges of life.

STOP AND ASK

Have you ever followed the directions of a map or a GPS to the tee and still found yourself lost? Yes, me too.

What do you do when the place you're looking for is not there and just can't seem to be found? You stop and ask for help. Sometimes we're too proud to ask for assistance and it usually cost us in the end. The truth is somebody has already been where you're trying to go and that means that person probably knows the way. So, don't ever be afraid to ask.

We should also not be afraid to ask God for help when we've gotten confused or have lost our way. Remember, He always knows the way because He always is the way.

> *James 1:5 – If any of you lack wisdom, let him ask of God, that giveth to all [men] liberally, and upbraideth not; and it shall be given him. But let him ask in faith, nothing wavering. For he that wavereth is like a wave of the sea driven with the wind and tossed.*

Whether we admit it or not, sometimes we just don't know. Sometimes, we lack the wisdom needed to get to where we're trying to go. This is where our Heavenly Father comes in. There's no sin in asking the One who knows everything about anything, especially your future. God answers those who call on Him and He gives to those who ask of Him.

Whenever we would go on a road trip, we would always have to factor in our travel expenses, especially the fuel costs. But, as we travel life's journey, the wisdom and knowledge needed is absolutely free. God gives us as much as we want and it's all FREE. What would you do if you were offered free gas, free oil changes, and free vehicle maintenance for the rest of your life? You would take it. You would also probably scream, "Thank You Jesus!" as loud as you could!

> *Jeremiah 33:3, "Call unto me, and I will answer thee, and shew thee great and mighty things, which thou knowest not."*

Do you hear what God is saying? He's giving you permission to call on Him when you're afraid, whenever you're unsure, whenever you feel lost, or whenever you just don't know the way.

I believe sometimes we think we bother, impose upon, or somehow inconvenience God when we call out to Him. But, we could never worry or weary the Everlasting God. The Father promises to respond to us if we are willing to reach out to Him. Look at the rest of the verse. He says He will show us great and mighty things about ourselves, things that we have no knowledge of. Did you realize that there are great and mighty things about you and your destiny that only God can reveal? Yes, you, and God wants to tell you all about them. So don't be afraid to ask.

My parents are the most generous people that I've ever known. I believe that there's nothing that I could ever ask them for that they would not give, if they had it, and it was within reason. Why would they do this? Because they love me! Perhaps many of you have parents who are the same way. Well if our earthly parents have no problem blessing us when we ask, how much more will our Heavenly bless us when we ask Him? God has put everything we need in His Word. His Word is filled with His promises, and they all lead to our success.

I love reading poetry. I recently came across this poem that captures how God has given us the Bible to guide us through life, and to a very good life.

The Bible Is My Road Map

The Bible is my road map
Which guides me night and day;
It keeps me from a wrong turn
When I start to go astray.

If directions are confusing,
Or a caution sign appears,
I search the Bible scriptures
For the rightful way to steer.
It directs me through dry valleys,

Over bridges high and low,
By the fields of fresh green meadows,
Towards the plains of harvest gold.
As I reach my destination,
I thank the Lord above
For my mountaintop and road map
And His everlasting love.

Author - Key Blake-Medley

We all were created to go somewhere and to do something wonderful with our lives. And yes, that includes you. It is not God's will that any of us stumble through life without a plan or a purpose in mind.

Because of this, the Bible is that unique road map that tells us where we are, where we've been, where we're going, and how to get there. If we would just take the time to open it up and read it, we would be quite surprised with where it can take us.

CHAPTER THREE

FULLY EQUIPPED

Equipped: *To furnish or provide with whatever is needed for use or for any undertaking.*

You already have everything you need! Yes, you really do. My wife, Candace, and I went to Cancun, Mexico for our honeymoon. On day three, we scheduled a cruise to the beautiful Island of Cozumel. Upon arriving at the departure site for the forty-five minute excursion, we noticed the captain walking around the ship talking to some of his crew members in Spanish. We asked our personal guide what was going on. He said that the captain was checking on several things. He was verifying that there was enough food to accommodate all of the passengers. He wanted to be sure that there was an adequate amount of raft boats and life jackets for everyone in the case of an emergency.

And finally, he wanted to make sure that his vessel was mechanically safe and structurally sound enough to make the round trip voyage. Once the captain was certain and satisfied that all systems were a go, we set sail for our anticipated destination.

What about your life's journey? Are you prepared and equipped? Remember, although it's your destination, the Lord is sponsoring the trip. And this means He guarantees that you already have everything you need, even if you don't see it. There have been so many times when we have started out for a vacation or even just a short trip and suddenly realized that we forgot to pack something that we really needed. But this is never the case with our awesome and amazing God. He thinks of everything, which means nothing is ever left out or left behind.

The truth is, we are filled and made full in Jesus Christ. Paul makes this very clear in Scripture.

> *Colossians 2:10 – And ye are complete in him, which is the head of all principality and power.*

Life without the Lord is empty and pointless, but an authentic relationship with the Savior automatically equips us with everything we need for our expedition through life. In fact, our Heavenly Father provides us with an immeasurable, incalculable, inexhaustible, never-ending supply of His love and grace. Finding our way through life becomes much easier when we put our trust in the One who gives us life and provides everything we need for life.

II Peter 1:3 – "According as his divine power hath given unto us all things that pertain unto life and godliness, through the knowledge of him that hath called us to glory and virtue." God truly supplies all of our needs according to His riches in glory by Christ Jesus.

YOU HAVE THE HOLY SPIRIT

We have also been given the precious gift of the Holy Spirit to lead us to a life of victory and success. The Holy Spirit is like our modern day GPS, but so much better. GPS, for the believer, could stand for God's Positioning System. God positions us for greatness and success! And one of the primary ways He does this is through the power of the Holy Spirit. Your glorious destiny exists and the Holy Spirit knows exactly where it is and how to get you there. How is this? He knows everything, remember.

John16:13 – Howbeit when he, the Spirit of truth, is come, he will guide you into all truth: for he shall not speak of himself; but whatsoever he shall hear, that shall he speak: and he will shew you things to come.

The pressure of having to figure out life, where to go, and what to do next is eliminated when we invite the Spirit of the Living God to lead the way.

Jesus promised that the Holy Ghost would escort us to the truth and show us what's down the road even before we get there. No more guessing or traveling down dead end streets; we have HELP. The Holy Ghost has the power and the insight to get us where we need to be. The key, however, is our willingness to allow Him. How good are you at listening to Him?

> *John 14:26 – But the Comforter, which is the Holy Ghost, whom the Father will send in my name, he shall teach you all things, and bring all things to your remembrance, whatsoever I have said unto you.*

Sometimes in life we become frustrated, confused, disoriented, and even lost. When this happens we must follow the advice given by the prophet Isaiah.

> *Isaiah 30:21 – And thine ears shall hear a word behind thee, saying, This is the way, walk ye in it, when ye turn to the right hand, and when ye turn to the left.*

God's will for you on earth is always first dispatched from heaven. Therefore, your success in life will not come by the hands of human might and strength, but, "by My Spirit, saith the Lord of hosts." The Holy Ghost manifests and activates the Word of God concerning you. He is the trigger, the energizer, and the switch that turns on the promises that the Lord has made to us all. It is the responsibility of the Holy Spirit to lead us to our destiny and He will if we're willing to follow Him.

The same Spirt that raised Jesus from the dead is also able to lead you to a blessed and bright future. The Holy Ghost is the unseen presence and power of God who wants to work with you, for you, and in you. Hallelujah!

YOU HAVE OTHER PEOPLE

Sometimes, others can show us the way simply because they've already been where we're trying to go. And, sometimes, other people can show us the way because God has told them to help us. The Lord not only equips us with the Holy Spirit, but He also provides us with righteous men and women who can bless us along our way.

Don't ever hesitate to fill up your spiritual gas tank with the good instruction and aid from wise counselors and godly advisors. Many times in life, we're faced with decisions and choices that are not so easy to make on our own. We read our Bibles and pray for direction, but still feel uncertain and unsure about which way we should go. In times like these, it can be very helpful to seek the counsel of Spirit-filled, God-fearing people.

> *Proverbs 11:14 – Where no counsel is, the people fall: but in the multitude of counsellors there is safety.*

It is never out of order to ask for the advice and prayers of people who love the Lord. In fact, many times the Lord will strategically place people in our path with messages of instruction, encouragement and hope. When this is the case, we must be willing to stop, listen and learn.

With this being said, we must still proceed with some caution. Why? Because the devil also drops his own agents of evil along the roadways of life with the hopes of wrecking us and stopping us from reaching our destination. Listen to what Solomon said.

> *Proverbs 12:5 –"The thoughts of the righteous are right: but the counsels of the wicked are deceit."*

Before seeking consultation from others, it is important that we first examine their values and their character. This is important because the Bible says, "The way of a fool is right in his own eyes: but he that hearkeneth unto counsel is wise." Seeking wise counsel and godly advice is not a sign of weakness, but rather proof of maturity and humility.

Our knowledge of God's word and guidance from His Spirit will help us to discern the difference between wise and unwise counsel. At the end of the day, we don't necessarily put our trust in people, but we put our trust in God who uses people to help us on our journey through life.

YOU HAVE YOU

Whenever we're in the market for a new car, we generally shop for a vehicle that's fully loaded. This simply means that the automobile is equipped with an abundance of options which includes a lot of stuff that we need and a whole lot of stuff that we don't need. Well, a vehicle can have all the options, and gadgets in the world, but without a driver all of those bells and whistles are meaningless. And that's where you come in.

God has fully equipped you for your journey, but don't forget He has also equipped you with YOU. That's right. Without you, there's not even a need for the journey. With the help of God, you can be anything you want to be and you can do anything you want to do. So aim yourself in the direction of something big and somewhere big, and get ready to go there.

Writing to the church at Philippi, the apostle Paul stated," I can do all things through Christ which strengthens me." Of course, this is not to nullify what the Lord can do. For we know that it is our faith in God that causes us to have faith in ourselves. God has given each of us a voice, a smile, a mind, gifts, hope, dreams, ability, faith, direction and so much more. So, have faith in you, believe in you and be confident in you so you can do what you need to do and go where He wants you to go.

This can happen as you begin to see yourself as God sees you. Knowing that your identity, strength and confidence are all in the Lord will give you the courage needed to face the journey ahead of you. Without self-confidence, your life is likely to become an accumulation of accidents, breakdowns and stalls. But with confidence, success will find you, and it's only a matter of time.

Here are a few keys that will keep you on the right road to success.

1. Master being you — Set out to just be you, that's all. Strive to be the best you that you can be. We always fail at life when we attempt to be someone other than ourselves. People will like you and even love you for being you, not somebody else. God made you different on purpose. You would be surprised at what God can do through your uniqueness when you give Him a chance.

> *I Corinthians 15:10a –"By the grace of God*
> *I am what I am"*

That's right; you are who you are, whoever that is. And in order to make the most of yourself, you must be yourself. To try and be somebody else is to be nobody at all. Just be yourself, and believe in yourself. Learn how to celebrate you. You were fearfully and wonderfully made by the God of this universe. You are unique. You are an original and a one-of-a-kind. You are the real deal. So, talk like you and sing like you. Pray, work, act, live, and think like you because nobody on the planet can beat you when it comes to being you.

2. Don't compare yourself to others — Comparing yourself to other people is a setup and trap for disaster. The comparison game will make you insecure, lower your self-esteem, rob you of your joy, slow you down, cause you to doubt yourself and your God, and keep you from discovering and appreciating your own gifts and purpose in life.

> *Galatians 6:4 – Pay careful attention to your own work, for then you will get the satisfaction of a job well done, and you won't need to compare yourself to anyone else. - NLT*

We will never be satisfied with who we are if we are always comparing ourselves to somebody else. We will never grow or blossom into what God created us to be if our eyes are always on somebody else. We cannot allow someone else's looks, abilities, intelligence, skills, or success to throw us off track. So when you come across someone who is more successful than you, or better looking than you, or smarter than you… just thank God for them and then thank God for you.

3. Only say what God says about you — Always speak positively about yourself. Scripture teaches us that "life and death is in the power of the tongue."

If we speak negative words over ourselves, we will get negative results. But if we speak the Word of God over our lives on a daily basis, we open the door for the supernatural to take place. You are who the Word says you are. You have what the Word says you can have. And you can do what the Word says you can do. Now, start saying it because profession brings possession!

4. Be willing to accept your weaknesses — Yes, that's exactly what I said; learn to accept your weaknesses. We should never waste our weaknesses because the God who made us can always use them.

This may not be a popular concept because we usually want to do things in our own strength which gives us a feeling of self-sufficiency. On the other hand, we often try and hide or disguise our weaknesses, as well. But we don't have to do this because, although our insufficiencies bring us to the end of ourselves, they also lead us to the beginning of God and His amazing strength.

> *2 Corinthians 12:9-10 – But he said to me, "My grace is sufficient for you, for my power is made perfect in weakness." Therefore I will boast all the more gladly about my*

weaknesses, so that Christ's power may rest on me. [10] That is why, for Christ's sake, I delight in weaknesses, in insults, in hardships, in persecutions, in difficulties. For when I am weak, then I am strong. – NIV

It's natural for us to want to identify and celebrate our strengths. But I think that it is also helpful for us to realize and accept our weaknesses. Believe it or not some of our weaknesses were never meant for us to overcome. Some were designed by God so that His grace and mercy may be seen and magnified in our lives. We need to accept the fact that some of our weaknesses are simply for the glory of God. Now we can understand how it really is alright to be transparent before the Lord and people. I believe that God can and will do wonderful things for us even in the presence of our weaknesses. His great purpose and strength are usually born out of those weaknesses.

As you continue on, confront every one of your challenges on life's highway with the revelation of who you are in the Lord. You are redeemed. You are an overcomer, and you are a conqueror. The Lord has so carefully and thoughtfully prepared us for victory and triumph in life. By His grace and mercy, we've been fully equipped with everything we need to accomplish our purpose and His plan for our lives.

Chapter Four

Move To The Passenger Seat

Passenger: A traveler in a vehicle who bears no responsibility for the tasks required for that vehicle to arrive at its destination.

As you begin the journey of discovering your purpose for life, please know and understand that you're not traveling alone. The God of this universe does not send us to our destination, but He travels there with us. Country, super star singer, Kari Underwood, released a hit song in 2005 called "Jesus Take The Wheel."

The song was about a woman seeking help from the Lord as she lost control of her vehicle while traveling on an ice slicked road. She knew that her only hope for surviving this highway emergency was to invite Jesus to take control of her car. That's exactly what we should do. We should move over to the passenger's seat and allow the Lord to do the driving.

No matter how well we think we can drive, God's driving is always better than ours. The Lord knows so much more than we do when it comes to the ends and outs of life. He is aware of everything that's up the road and everything that's around the corner.

If we're going to reach our destination, now is the time to turn over the controls to God. Why? Because He knows the way, His vision is perfect, and there is absolutely nothing on earth that could ever stop Him or get in His way.

LET GO

I've always liked Greyhound Bus Line's slogan, at least their slogan at one time. It said, "Go Greyhound and leave the driving to us." The idea behind their catchy slogan was that they'll do everything necessary to get you where you're going, on time, and all you need to do is just ride. You don't have to worry about road conditions, falling asleep at the wheel, stressful construction zones, irate drivers, or getting a speeding ticket from Steve the State Trooper. Give them control and your only responsibility will be to ride.

For many of us, it's quite difficult to let go and surrender control of our lives to a God we cannot see. As human beings, we love the idea of having control over things, people, situations and life in general. We love power, which essentially is control. But as believers, we must grow to the place where we trust that God absolutely knows what's best for us. We think we know. We love our plans that we plan. But letting go means surrendering ourselves and our plans to God and His perfect will.

> *Matthew 16:24 – Then said Jesus unto his disciples, If any man will come after me, let him deny himself, and take up his cross, and follow me.*

Sometimes, not letting go is the one thing that keeps us from going on. So, we must learn to surrender, which is a sign that we trust the Lord with everything. Here's what letting go and surrendering to God looks like:

- We wait for God's timing, although, we're not sure when it will come.

- We trust God's purpose no matter the circumstances.

- We follow God's lead even when He refuses to tell us where we're going.

- We rely on God to work things out instead of trying to manipulate and control the situation.

- We trust God more instead of trying to work harder to make things happen.

I think the main reason we should have no problems with letting go is because most of the time we just don't know what we're doing. Really, we don't. We may not have the courage to admit it, but it's true anyway. How many times have we gone down the wrong road or taken the wrong turn in life because we thought we knew the way? Probably too many to remember. Then, what happens? We're left with frustration and irritation because once again, we have to re-route. Let's just admit it right now, it will always be in our best interest to allow the Lord to take the lead. Let's admit that we are weak, but He is strong and we will always need His assistance. Listen to what Jesus said:

> *John 5:30 – I can of mine own self do nothing: as I hear, I judge: and my judgment is just; because I seek not mine own will, but the will of the Father which hath sent me.*

There's somewhere God's wants you to go and something He wants you to do. And you can't accomplish it on your own; you will need His help. Good news! God wants to help you; He really does. But He can't help you if you don't surrender and give Him control. If you really want to enjoy a rich and satisfying life, let go. Letting go is the only way we can let God take the wheel of our lives.

LET GOD

When we totally give our lives over to the Lord, the Holy Spirit will take control and lead us to our purpose and destination. One thing I've learned in life is that God knows what He's doing. He has the experience and a proven track record of nothing but success. He controls all of the resources of not only His Kingdom, but of the world. Everything that's anything and anywhere belongs to the Lord and is at His immediate disposal for our assistance. We need the strength, guidance and ability that only God can provide. Our God not only specializes at being God, but He also specializes at helping us.

> *Isaiah 41:13 – For I am the Lord, your God,*
> *who takes hold of your right hand and says to*
> *you, Do not fear; I will help you.*

If you have grown weary of traveling, He can help you. If you've lost your way, He can help you. If the road map to your destiny has become blurry and confusing, God can help you. He says so right there in the verse, "I will help you." His help is personal. We know this is true because the scripture says that He reaches out His hand to touch our hand and that's personal. Jehovah's helping hand indicates that He's familiar with us and that He's friends with us. This frees us from having to worry or be fearful about any enemy that may be following us. We're safe when our hands are in the hands of our Heavenly Father. His divine affection towards us reminds us that we belong to Him and that He only desires the best for us.

Sometimes, we'll come upon roads that have been closed and detours that take us way out of the way, but, even then, He makes us this promise:

Psalm 32:8 – I will instruct thee and teach thee in the way which thou shalt go: I will guide thee with mine eye.

This is what happens when we have the courage to let go and let God. He makes Himself, His hands and His eyes available to us at all times.

We're reminded that the One who knows the way and shows us the way is the Way. What do you need God to help you with? I suggest making a list. Don't worry about how long or exhausting it may be, just make it. Make it and then ask Him to help you with it. Don't allow selfish pride to keep you from reaching out for help from the One who can always help. With your eyes, look for Him. With your hands, feel for Him, and with your heart, trust in Him. There is nothing wrong with riding on the passenger side of life, especially when you know the Lord is doing the driving.

GET SOME REST

On a recent trip to Chattanooga, I received an ego boost from my wife that left me blushing from ear to ear and feeling really good. Forty five minutes after leaving home, Candace asked me if I wanted her to drive, and as always my answer was, "No, I'm alright." She then reached over and kissed me on my cheek and told me how much she loved and appreciated me. She said, "You've really spoiled me; I never have to drive when we go on these trips. It's like all I have to do is sit back, relax, rest, and just ride. Thank you so much."

This is what God does for us, a thousand times over, when we voluntarily move to the passenger seat. When we let go of the wheel of life and give Him full control, we can rest as we go. A natural rest will occur when we commit ourselves to allowing the Lord to do the driving. We really need to learn to trust and rest in our Heavenly Father's love and the plan He has for our lives.

> *Psalms 37:7 – "Rest in the Lord, and wait patiently for him."*

Too often, we find ourselves inundated with trying to plot and plan the next step of our lives and every step thereafter. Satan loves it when we do this. He knows that when we try to run and control every aspect of our lives, it keeps us from fully trusting the promises of God, and it keeps us from resting in Him.

The truth of the matter is the Lord never intended for us, or gave us the responsibility of knowing all the answers to our future. And we've got to believe that God works best when we're at rest. That is resting in Him and trusting that He has everything under control. This is exactly what David is talking about in this next text.

Psalm 46:10 – Be still and know that I am God.

Do you know that God is God? Do you trust Him to be your father and to take care of your every need? If so, you can rest. I mean really rest… the kind of rest that has no worries. You see, when we can breathe, relax and rest in the Lord, it shows Him that we trust Him and that we're ready to receive the good things from Him that this world could never give us. A life of peace and joy can only be ours as we trust and receive the Lord's sweet rest.

Rest is a place of surrender and submission that creates an environment for our trust in God to flourish and grow. Restlessness, on the other hand, often brings on frustration, anxiety, anger, insecurity, and fear. But God's love for us and our faith in Him eliminates restlessness and all that comes with it. Rest, then, reminds us that we don't have to always be in control. In fact, there will never be an occasion in your life when God will need you to help Him be in control. The One who supervises the universe is more than able and capable to manage your life.

So, move to the passenger seat, sit back, relax, get some rest, and just enjoy the ride. God knows exactly what He's doing, and exactly where He's going.

CHAPTER FIVE

LOCATE THE GLORY

Glory: High renowned praise, honor, dignity, majesty, greatness, and worship that is attributed to God.

My first automobile was a 1968 Chevy Nova. It was black on blue with four in the floor. I was sixteen and ready to roll. But before my father gave me the keys, he gave me the speech - The NO Speech... "No fast driving, no wild friends, no drugs, no alcohol, no overcrowding, no running out of gas, no loud music, no racing, and no one else is to ever drive your car. And no doing or going anywhere in this car where you're not supposed to." What my dad was really saying was that my car was only to be used for good. He was also saying that I'd better not mess up and make him or my mom look bad by doing something foolish in my new, old car.

In this chapter, you will be challenged to locate the glory. That is, will what you want to do and be in life please God? Will it make Him happy and facilitate your reason for living? Will your goals and aspirations allow you to live for the glory of God? And just what does living for the glory of God really mean anyway?

It means we go all out and all the way for Jesus. It means that for Christ's sake, we hold nothing back and we invest everything we have, including ourselves in Him and His Kingdom. God's glory is His presence growing in us through His Son and our Savior Jesus Christ. As the Lord's character increases in us, we decrease, showing forth God's character of grace, love, truth, goodness and hope. This glorious life that He gives us is what gives us the power to live for Him.

BRING ON THE GLORY

As you set out to fulfill your purpose in creation, always strive to honor the Creator in all that you do.

By doing this, you can experience a good life, one that is filled with joy and surprises, hope and happiness, and promise and potential. We must know that our real reason for existing is to fellowship with and serve God. This is why we were born and this is what living for the glory of God is all about. Decide right now, that by the grace of God, you're going to live the rest of your life for the glory of God.

> *2 Corinthians 5:9 – We make it our goal to please him, whether we are at home in the body or away from it. NIV*

1 Corinthians 10:31 – Whether therefore ye eat, or drink, or whatsoever ye do, do all to the glory of God.

The goals we set in life should cause us to trust God more and this always brings glory to our Heavenly Father. When we make it our business to glorify the Lord, He gets involved and helps us to accomplish our goals.

How do you know if you're bringing glory to God? If your aspirations in life cause you to love God more, trust God more, obey God more, worship God more, and serve God more, then you know you're on the right road to glorifying God. If you can get God to bless, sanction, give a thumbs up, or participate in your next decision or your next move, then you know you're on the right road to glorifying God.

Everything we do in life should be about bringing glory to God. Let's look at a quick short list of how we should be glorifying our God.

WE SHOULD GLORIFY GOD…

By what we do
Our actions and deeds in life should be a reflection of the One who gave us this new life; His name is Jesus. When people see us, they should also see the Lord shinning in us and shining through us. The Lord taught us to, "Let your light so shine before men, that they may see your good works and glorify your Father which is in heaven." The light should always be on, because people are always watching. So make it your business to represent Him well by allowing your light to shine as bright as it can.

By the way we think
If we intend to glorify God, our thoughts, emotions and feelings must be immersed in the Word of God and controlled by the Holy Spirit at all times. We must remember that who we are on the outside is a reflection of who we are on the inside. Cast down every thought and imagination that would not be pleasing to God.

With what we say
As children of God, we must become well versed in the Word of God. What we say to and about others should always, in some way, bring glory to God. We avoid words that are critical, harsh, abusive, insulting, demeaning, or hurtful. We avoid gossip and dirty jokes. We use faith-filled words that bring life and not death.

With our attitude

People can be turned on or off by our attitude, they can be encouraged or discouraged by our attitude. The right attitude will lead us to the right altitude. According to scripture, our attitude towards life, circumstances, others, and even ourselves should be like the Lord's.

Philippians 2:5 – "Let this mind be in you, which was also in Christ Jesus."

Good attitudes demonstrate being positive, encouraging, loving, humble, teachable, cooperative, considerate, selfless, loyal and persevering, which all bring glory to God.

With our bodies

The way we treat others is important, but the way we treat ourselves is just as important. Our bodies are temples and they house the Holy Spirit; therefore, we must keep them clean and holy. We must also take care of our bodies by keeping them strong and healthy. Of course we do this by not overindulging in anything. We also do it by eating heathy, getting plenty of exercise, drinking lots of water, abstaining from drugs, alcohol and tobacco. Paul reminds us in Scripture to, "Glorify God with our bodies which belong to the Lord."

In our relationships

Relationships are a crucial part of life; therefore, we must sincerely do our part to build, maintain and restore them. As believers, we should practice treating each other the way the Lord has treated us. God is always glorified when we're about the business of building strong relationships with our families, friends, neighbors, and especially our brothers and sisters in Christ.

In our work

This includes our jobs, education, homes, businesses and volunteering. Prospering in our finances, growing in our knowledge and serving humanity are all supported by scripture and can bring glory to God. However, we must never allow any of those good things to become greater than God. We worship and bow down to the Creator and not His creation. Our work, assignments, callings and responsibilities in life should always be unveiling and showcasing the awesome, magnificent glory of God.

In our recreation

Yes, God wants us to glorify Him even when we play, and yes God has no problem with us playing. However, we must be very careful about what we play, how we play, and when we play. We must allow our minds to feed on that which wholesome an honoring to God.

Television programs, books, movies, concerts, plays, sports, music and social media can all be very entertaining. But we should never allow any of these things to cause us to compromise our morals or who we are in Christ. Even when it comes to our friends, we must remain true to our God by conducting ourselves in a manner which makes Him smile.

At all times

It's not hard to praise and glorify God when all is well in our lives. But can we do it during times of testing and trials? We're called to glorify God when we're experience difficulties, setbacks, suffering and sadness.

In fact, glorifying the Father in the midst of struggles strengthens our relationship with the Lord and causes others to put their trust in God as they witness Him walking with us during our tough times.

SEEK GOD'S HEART

Living for the glory of God means we seek to know and have His heart. More than anything else in life, we seek to become more like Him. We seek to know His heart so that our heart may be like His. You see, we cannot fully know God if we don't know the heart of God. The heart of God is unconditional love, compassion and goodwill toward all men. That's what God wants from us. He wants us to have a heart like His heart, and He wants us to seek His heart with our whole heart. Do you remember in the Old Testament when God rejected King Saul? Well, He did so because Saul disobeyed Him and did not have His heart. Paul talked about Saul's heart problem in the New Testament.

> *Acts 13:22 – But God removed Saul and replaced him with David, a man about whom God said, 'I have found David son of Jesse, a*

man after my own heart. He will do every-
thing I want him to do. - NLT

God just wants people who will do what He wants them to do. He wants someone who will listen to Him intently, and obey without reservation. He wants somebody who will be humble enough to show true compassion and genuine kindness. He desires a people who will show goodwill towards everybody, even those who are considered to be nobody. This is the heart of God.

What does it mean to be a person after God's own heart? It means our lives are in sync with the Lord. It means we are deeply sensitive to spiritual things and the things that please Him. It means we go where He wants us to go and do what He wants us to do. It means His plan becomes our purpose in life and for life.

> *2 Chronicles 16:9 – "For the eyes of Yahweh roam throughout the earth to show Himself strong for those whose hearts are completely His." - HCSB*

God is looking for people who will love Him and serve Him with their whole heart and not just a piece of it. We can never fool or bamboozle the Living God. He's not merely impressed with our externals, but He searches and focuses on the internal, that which is in our hearts. The character of our hearts tells of who we are and where we're going. When our hearts begin to beat to the same rhythm of the heartbeat of God, then we will know that we are indeed living for the glory of God.

CONTINUE TO LIVE FOR CHRIST

Some of my colleagues and I made our way to a convention in Nashville, Tennessee where we were to be honored for exceptional work we had performed. We were employed by a well-known national company. There were other systems from around the country that were being honored as well. That first night they threw a big party for us, and that's when I overheard a very powerful conversation. A man was telling his co-worker, neither of which I knew, to relax and let her hair down, and enjoy herself.

He said, nobody here knows you; you can get drunk, party, get wild, live it up, do what you want to do, and no one will ever know what happened. She responded, but I don't do those things at home so why would I do them here. Then she said, "Plus God would know."

We must remember, no matter what we do or where we go in life, as believers we are the Lord's ambassadors. We represent God, the Kingdom of God, and Heaven's business on earth.

> *2 Corinthians 5:20 – "Now then we are ambassadors for Christ"*

We are Christ's representatives in this world. He uses us to persuade men and women to be saved, delivered, and set free. He uses us, our names, and our reputations to get us where He wants us to be, and where we really need to be. Therefore, we are to let our lights shine by modeling the fruits of the Spirit, walking in holiness, kindness, and forgiveness. This is living for the glory of God. Again, people are watching us. They watch the way we walk, the way we talk, the way we respond, the way we love, and the way we do business for God. The world that we've been called to lead to Christ is forever checking us out.

As ambassadors of Jesus Christ, we must remember we no longer represent our own interests, agendas, wishes or wants. And we no longer represent ourselves. Why? Because we no longer belong to ourselves. Paul reminds us of this:

> *1 Corinthians 6:20 – For you are bought with*
> *a price: therefore glorify God in your body,*
> *and in your spirit, which are God's.*

Our lives and our lifestyles must become living testimonies to the glory of God and the power of Jesus Christ, thereby producing godliness and goodness for all to see.

Whatever is of God will also reflect the glory of God. God is glorified, magnified and satisfied when we produce fruits of righteousness.

John 15:8 – Herein is my Father glorified, that ye bear much fruit; so shall ye be my disciples.

The fruit we produce is not strife or contention; it's not arrogance or pride; it's not division or hostility; it's not selfishness or self-righteousness; it's not anger or animosity; and its most certainly not doubt or fear.

But the fruit we produce is peace, unity, brotherly love, kindness, reconciliation, hope, forgiveness, honor, friendship, joy, support, encouragement and faith. This kind of fruit expresses the heart of God.

As you continue to allow Christ to work out His purposes in your life, glorifying God will become your lifestyle. Look for His glory in all you do. If you can locate those things that bring honor and glory to your Heavenly Father, you're on the right path. If you cannot find the glory, stop. Stop and look around, and then turn around, because you're probably headed in the wrong direction.

CHAPTER SIX

LET'S GO

Go: To move from one place or point to another.

As a child, and even now I love go-kart racing. I recall in my teenage years, going to an amusement park in Florida one year and standing in line for hours to participate in a race that would only last for about eight minutes. To this day, I remember that little girl in front me who promised that she was going to beat me. She went on and on about how she was going to leave me in her dust. Finally, we were strapped in our karts and given the green light to go. And then something strange happened, actually nothing happened at all. The girl who did all that bragging just sat there. Her dad yelled, "Go Kelly Go! Mash the gas and go." But she never did, she never moved. As I topped the hill I saw the attendants taking her out of her go-kart and she was crying. Turns out Kelly was scared. She was afraid that she would crash, or get bumped too hard, or not win the race, so she just sat there and didn't move.

Sadly, many people are the same way in life. They never reach their goals, or discover their true potential because they are afraid to go. Fear of failure and even fear of the future can keep us right where we are. We must remember that the journey of a thousand miles or just a few feet always begins with the first step. If we ever expect to get there, where ever there may happen to be, we've got to first get going. We have to move. The possibility of progress always exists where there is positive movement.

GOD HAS PAVED THE WAY

God has taken on the full responsibility of guiding our foot-steps to our place of destiny. We don't have to burden our-selves with having to know the exact what, when, where, and how's of life. Instead we can turn the reigns of our lives over to God, and let Him order our steps. No matter where you're going, God has already been there, cleared a path, and paved the way for you to get there.

> *Jeremiah 29:11 – "For I know the plans I have for you," says the Lord. "They are plans for good and not for disaster, to give you a future and a hope. - NLT*

God knows what's best for you, and He is fully aware that what you can be in life is much greater than you can ever imagine. Why? Because He's the One who created the blue-print for your life. He has carefully thought out and thought through your life, not leaving out one single detail. Your existence and success are both important to Him. The Lord does not have a plan for your life, He has "The Plan" for your life. God wrote the book on you, and it's a good book with a happy ending.

There are so many roads, streets, avenues, and highways in life and sometimes choosing the right one can be very difficult. But it really doesn't have to be that way if we allow God to be our guide. Remember the Lord knows the way because He is the way.

> *Psalm 32:8 – I will instruct you and teach you*
> *in the way you should go; I will guide you*
> *with my eye.*

Isn't it wonderful to know that the God of this universe has His eyes on us and where we're going? He leads us and counsels us out of His perfect knowledge of all things. His instruction keeps us from going astray, and from going the wrong way. Hallelujah, thank you Jesus! The Bible makes it clear that the Lord has paved the way to a good life for His children right here on earth. Our job is to trust in Him and not ourselves. God has promised to direct the paths of our lives, and where there are no paths He will create some.

The steps of a good man or a good woman are indeed ordered by the Lord. Our responsibility now is to live each day to the best of our ability; loving God, listening to God, and living for God, by following God.

SEE YOURSELF ALREADY THERE

As a child I always looked forward to going to Six Flags in Atlanta, Georgia. It was the summer trip that my sisters and I longed for all year long. We would talk about what we were going to ride. We would go on and on about how many times we would ride the water logs and the roller coasters. I can remember imagining myself there at the amusement park even before I got there. I know that may sound silly and childish, but I did.

I really think we should have the same attitude about our goals and what we want to accomplish in life. By faith you must see yourself in your place of purpose long before you get there. For believers this means that victory begins in the mind. We must learn how to use the power of our imagination. We must learn to imagine being there, being happy, being healed, being promoted, and being blessed. One of the most powerful tools that God has given the human race is the human mind. And He wants us to use our mind and our imagination to see ourselves beyond where we are right now.

> *Genesis 11:6 – And the Lord said, "Behold, the people is one, and they have all one language; and this they begin to do: and now nothing will be restrained from them, which they have imagined to do."*

In this verse the God of the universe makes a very powerful confession, "And now nothing will be restrained from them, which they have imagined to do." We eventually move in the direction of our most dominant thoughts and beliefs. Albert Einstein said, "Your imagination is your preview of life's coming attractions." Jesus Christ said, "All things are possible to him who believes!"

What are you thinking, believing, and imagining? Imagine yourself in a happy place, a righteous place, a good place, a wealthy place, and in a successful place. You can lose the weight if you think you can. You can start a business if you think you can. You can make a difference if you think you can. I thought I could write this book, and I did, and now you're reading it.

Seeing yourself in the place of your purpose will require that you protect your imagination by controlling your thoughts. Thoughts from everywhere and from all directions will constantly try to invade your imagination, so you must protect it. How? We protect our mind by flooding and saturating it with the Word of God. The Bible says, "as a man thinks in his heart, so is he." Again, we usually go the way of our most dominant thinking. We become what we think we will.

So we must constantly read and speak God's faith filled words over our lives, situations, and circumstances. By the same token we must reject what Satan says about us.

Dismiss and reject evil and negative thoughts and words from entering into your heart and spirit.

> *2 Corinthians 10:5 – Casting down imaginations, and every high thing that exalteth itself against the knowledge of God, and bringing into captivity every thought to the obedience of Christ;*

There will be many things and thoughts that will try to knock Christ down from the pedestal of your heart. Cast them down. Cast down anger, bitterness, and jealousy. Cast down fear, doubt, and worry. Cast down lust, dishonesty, and cheating. Cast down foolishness, idleness, disobedience, and evil of every kind. In fact, be ready to cast down any and everything that will keep you from reaching your destiny, and being a winner in life.

GOD IS GOING WITH YOU

I remember the very first time I flew on an air plane. I was terrified. No I was horrified! As the time drew closer for us to return home I remember hoping and praying that my parents would choose a different mode of transportation to get us back to Alabama that did not include flying. But they didn't. As we arrived at the airport that morning, I remember feeling sick to my stomach. I thought, "Why can't we just ride the bus home, like we rode the bus out here?" Here being Los Angeles, California. And then as we began boarding the plane the Lord spoke these words to me. I was only thirteen years old but I know it was God. He said, "Don't worry, I'm with you." And then He said it again, "Don't worry, I'm with you." All of sudden I felt at peace and my fear was gone. As we began to taxi down the runway and soar into the air the fear retuned, and this time it was even greater. And then the Lord said this, "Don't worry, I'm still with you." My fear went away and I was relaxed the rest of the flight because I believed that God was indeed with me.

It is comforting to know that no matter where we go in life, God has promised to go with us. Sometimes you may find yourself in dark places or impossible situations, but rest assured, God is there with you, paying close attention to you. He walks with you every moment of every day. God is with you, loving you, leading you, protecting you, providing for you, and guiding you with His presence. This is great news!

As we travel through life, we know we're not traveling alone. God is with us. The Amplified version of Hebrews 13:5 makes it clear that God is continually with us.

> *Hebrews 13:5 – "...for He has said, "I will never [under any circumstances] desert you [nor give you up nor leave you without support, nor will I in any degree leave you helpless], nor will I forsake or let you down or relax My hold on you [assuredly not]!" - AMP*

Go back and slowly read that verse again. Those are shouting words! Hallelujah! Now feel free to take a thirty second praise break! God never leaves us or abandons us. He's always right there with us, with His never-ending supply of all that we need.

Whatever we need for life the Lord has it with Him. He has faith, healing, understanding, strength, peace, love, joy, hope, mercy, and grace. He has it all. Our God pours out His favor and blessing upon us through His ever abiding presence.

> *Psalm 16:11 – Thou wilt shew me the path of life: in thy presence is fullness of joy; at thy right hand there are pleasures for evermore.*

Again, everything we need for a successful journey through life is in God's presence. That's the key - His presence. If you're finding it difficult to sense the Lord's presence, it may be because your life has become too cluttered with the things of this life.

The family, the job, the bills, the meetings, the television, and social media, can all become distractions that keep us from hearing and seeing God. The remedy for this is to simply follow the advice that comes from the Bible that says, "Be still and know that I am God." That's right, settle down, sit down, and be still.

I also encourage you to read and meditate on the scriptures below. They will help to build your faith and remind you that God is always with you. Jesus said, "It is written, Man shall not live by bread alone, but by every word that proceedeth out of the mouth of God." In other words we cannot make it or be sustained by the things of this world alone. We need His word, and we need His truth, to lead and guide us through life.

Isaiah 58:11 – And the LORD shall guide thee continually, and satisfy thy soul in drought, and make fat thy bones: and thou shalt be like a watered garden, and like a spring of water, whose waters fail not.

Deuteronomy 31:8 – And the Lord, he it is that doth go before thee; he will be with thee, he will not fail thee, neither forsake thee: fear not, neither be dismayed.

Isaiah 41:10 – Fear thou not; for I am with thee: be not dismayed; for I am thy God: I will strengthen thee; yea, I will help thee; yea, I will uphold thee with the right hand of my righteousness.

Psalm 145:18 – "The Lord is close to all who call on him" - NLT

Matthew 28:20 – "Lo, I am with you always, even unto the end of the world."

God so desperately wants to be close to you as you make your way through life. As you draw near to Him, you will feel Him drawing closer and closer to you. As you go, be assured that the Lord is forever with you.

My prayer is that you will always sense the fullness of the Father's everlasting peace and love, as He graces you with His abiding presence.

Now, no more procrastinating. No more delaying. No more putting off, or postponing. No more waiting for perfect conditions. If you don't leave now you may never get there. It's time to get up and go. So let's do it, let's GO!

CHAPTER SEVEN

DRIVEN BY PASSION

Passion: Expressing a strong liking or desire for or devotion to some activity, object, or concept.

The first time I can ever really remember being passionate about anything was around the age of eleven. I had become fascinated and even obsessed with television, not necessarily watching it, but how it worked. It was always amazing to me how they got pictures and sound to come out of that square box. I was determined to find out, and my passion for telecommunications would drive me to find out. I did a lot of research, read a few books, and asked a thousand questions. I can remember opening up old television sets and exploring the inward parts. By the time I was a senior in high school, my passion for the subject matter had literally dropped me off at the local television. You can call it fate, but I knew it was God fulfilling my dream and rewarding my passion. Of all people, I was selected to participate in an internship through a program called VICA, Vocational Industrial Clubs of America. I initially signed up for this elective class as a joke, but little did I know at the time, it would be the starting point of a successful career for me in the television industry for the next decade and a half. I would go from being the all-around gopher and errand boy to the paid senior technical director and night manager at our local television station. I would later leave the TV station and accepted the position of director of television advertisement for the largest cable company in America. I owe a lot of that success to the passion that God put in me for television. I believe that passion can help take us all the way to where we're going in life.

God has given each one of us this gift called passion. It may be buried deep within you, but it's there. In fact your passion has always been there, waiting for you to discover it and to use it. So grab it and decide at this very moment in history, that you will never spend another second living a life that is not driven by purpose and passion.

> *Romans 12:11 – Never be lazy, but work hard and serve the Lord enthusiastically. – NLT*

> *Titus 2:14 – Who gave himself for us, that he might redeem us from all iniquity, and purify unto himself a peculiar people, zealous of good works.*

Nothing great in life will ever be accomplished without enthusiasm, zeal, and especially passion. Passion is like a fire on the inside that affects everything on the outside.

Passion is a driving force. It drove Jesus Christ past humiliation, suffering, and unbearable pain, all the way to the cross. Passion has driven biblical figures, civil rights leaders, humanitarians, scientists, preachers, missionaries, fathers, house moms, musicians, athletes, entrepreneurs, dreamers, and everyday people just like you, to achieve greatness in life. Passion is part of what makes our lives worth living, and even dying for. Passion compels us to act, and it urges us to get up, to get going, and to do something.

LOCATE YOUR PURPOSE

Purpose is the reason why something is created or exists. So then one of the first things you must do is find out why God created you, and what it is He wants you to do. The discovery of our purpose is what activates our passion. Without purpose life can become meaningless, boring, futile, and one big bother. The prophet Isaiah made a very somber confession about a period in his life, and oftentimes some of us may feel the same way.

> *Isaiah 49:4 – I replied, "But my work seems so useless! I have spent my strength for nothing and to no purpose. Yet I leave it all in*

the Lord's hand; I will trust God for my re-
ward." - NLT

An unclear and uncertain purpose will smother our passion. If we're not careful we'll spend a lifetime trying to figure out what we're supposed to be doing in life. We ask advice from family, friends, neighbors, and even sometimes from complete strangers. And when we're not asking others for their opinions, we simply guess at what we think our purpose in life should be. All of this is really unnecessary. Why? Because all we really have to do is go to the source, our Heavenly Father. Yes, we go to God, after all it is God who has placed His purpose within us. God always wants what's best for His children, and He always knows what's best for His children. He has the plans, and we must trust Him with His plans.

> *Jeremiah 29:11 – For I know the plans I have*
> *for you," says the Lord. "They are plans for*
> *good and not for disaster, to give you a future*
> *and a hope. – NLT*

> *James 1:5 – If any of you lacks wisdom [to*
> *guide him through a decision or circum-*
> *stance], he is to ask of [our benevolent] God,*
> *who gives to everyone generously and*

without rebuke or blame, and it will be given

to him. - AMP

There we have it; we have an open invitation to ask God for wisdom and understanding. What's keeping you from asking God for His help? What's keeping you from asking God for clarity, and for answers to the questions you have about your life? He holds the blue prints, and road maps to your future, and He will unveil it to you if you have the courage to ask Him. The greater your purpose in life, the more passionate you'll be about living it. Go ahead and commit yourself to the Lord's purpose for your life and He'll give you all the passion needed to fulfill that purpose.

IDENTIFY YOUR GIFTS

What can you do? What is it that you are absolutely good at? God has given each of us unique gifts, talents, and abilities. This is what makes us who we are and sets us apart from everyone else on the planet. Our passion then steps in and causes those gifts and abilities to be maximized and utilized to the fullest. We should never ignore the gifts and special abilities that God has given us, but rather we should use them for His glory.

1 Peter 4:10 – God has given each of you a gift from his great variety of spiritual gifts. Use them well to serve one another. – NLT

1 Corinthians 7:17 – Each of you should go on living according to the Lord's gift to you, and as you were when God called you. This is the rule I teach in all the churches. - GNT

Just like our purpose in life is not just about us, the same holds true when it comes to our gifts and talents. Our God-given abilities go far beyond becoming rich, or famous, or beloved by thousands. God blesses us with gifts so we can fulfil our purpose and be a blessing to others. Therefore we must be careful to use our gifts wisely and not selfishly.

1 Corinthians 4:2 – Now, a person who is put in charge as a manager must be faithful. - NLT

Have you ever thought about it like that? The Bible says that we are managers of the gifts and abilities that God has bestowed upon us. Our gifts are to be opened and used. That means there's no place for laziness, procrastination, slothfulness, or comparing your gifts to the gifts of others. To us our gifts may seem small and insignificant, but that's not the way our God feels at all. Every gift, no matter how big or small, is precious in His sight. So we must remain faithful to the investment the Lord has made in us. I believe that somewhere down the road that investment will pay great dividends, if we remain faithful and true. God makes us ruler over much when we prove to be faithful over little. Our passion will energize our talents and abilities as we purpose in our hearts to use them for the good, as well as for God's glory.

MANAGE YOUR TIME

There was a time in my life and in the life of my ministry when I thought I could do it all. I could help everyone, I could save everyone, I could serve everyone, I could care for everyone, I could meet with everyone, and I could rescue everyone. I remember thinking at one time that I could find the answer for everyone, I could pray for everyone, I could be there for everyone, and God forbid, if ever I said no to anyone. I know that's a mouthful, right? But that's just how I was living my life, and I'm afraid that I'm not alone in this struggle.

This may sound good and noble at first glance, but it's really a big, big problem. The problem is each person is only one person, and one person can only do so much. Sometimes we give out and burn out because we have not learned how to have balance in our lives. We have not yet mastered the art of properly managing our time. We can become so busy doing so much that we end up not doing much of anything at all. At least that's been the case with me.

I would like to offer a few helpful tips on how you can remain passionate while still balancing and managing your time for success. And yes, I will take my own advice, in this matter.

Tip #1 - Recognize God — Take time to recognize that God has created and gifted you to do His will, His work, His way. Ephesians 2:10 - For we are God's masterpiece. He has created us anew in Christ Jesus, so we can do the good things he planned for us long ago. – NLT Allowing God to do what He wants to do with us must become a high priority in our lives. Remember, God created you for Him!

Tip #2 - Take Responsibility — Assume responsibility for the use of your own time. Remember time waits on no one, not even you. Once it's gone it's gone and there's no getting it back. Ephesians 5:16 – Making the very most of your time [on earth, recognizing and taking advantage of each opportunity and using it with wisdom and diligence], because the days are [filled with] evil. – AMP Take control over your time as best as you can, and remember if you don't manage your time, someone else will manage your time for you.

Tip #3 - Plan Well — As it's been said, "people don't plan to fail they just fail to plan. Alan Lakin said, "Planning is bringing the future into the present so that you can do something about it now." Proverbs 16:3 - Commit to the LORD whatever you do, and he will establish your plans. – NIV The Bible also says in Proverbs 13:16, "A wise man thinks ahead; a fool doesn't and even brags about it!" – TLB Reaching goals and achieving success in life demands that we plan ahead. Planning ahead also helps to alleviate stress, opening the door for our passion to burst on the scene.

Key #4 - Organize and Prioritize — Too often our sched-
ules are crowded to the point that it seems impossible to do
all the things we need to do. So we must diligently organize
and prioritize all those duties, responsibilities, and activities
that fill our plates. Decide what's most important and commit to getting those things done first. Matthew 6:33 - But
seek ye first the kingdom of God, and his righteousness; and
all these things shall be added unto you. When we put God
first, everything else in life will fall right into place. Learn-
ing to prioritize and organize keeps us motivated, on track,
and on time. And never be afraid to eliminate those things
that are not important.

DEAL WITH YOUR SINS

Without a doubt unconfessed sin is a passion killer. Sin that
is not dealt with will rob us of joy, excitement, and enthusiasm. The same is true when there is unresolved conflict in
our lives, or when we refuse to forgive. These attitudes are
draining, and they leave little or no room for passion to exist,
or to do its job. Look at what the psalmist had to say about
what sin had done to him. Psalm 38:4-6 - My guilt has over-
whelmed me like a burden too heavy to bear. My wounds
fester and are loathsome because of my sinful folly. I am
bowed down and brought very low; all day long I go about
mourning. – NIV
But thanks to God there is a cure, and remedy for our sins. 1
John 1:9 - "If we confess our sins, God can be trusted to
forgive you our sins and to cleanse you from all unrighteous-
ness." We should always own up to our sins, and then give

them to God. Once we've confessed our sins, and repented of our sins, then God will forgive us for our sins. These actions put us right back on track, and with the power of passion, the journey continues.

We must also strive to keep our emotions in check. Negative emotions like jealousy, envy, resentment, rage, rebellion, bitterness, and uncontrolled anger, weakens the drive of passion. This is why it is so important to have and maintain a loving and forgiving spirit. Passion thrives in an environment like this.

MAKE ROOM FOR GOD AND OTHERS

At the end of the day passion is really a spiritual matter that has its roots deep in God, and because of this we must always make room for Him in our hearts. Nothing can bring out the passion that is on the inside of us the way God can. After all He's the one that put the passion in us in the first place. Jesus taught His disciples to embrace and love His Father with great passion. Matthew 22:37-40 - Jesus said, "'Love the Lord your God with all your passion and prayer and intelligence.' This is the most important, the first on any list. But there is a second to set alongside it: 'Love others as well as you love yourself.' These two commands are pegs; everything in God's Law and the Prophets hangs from them." – MSG We make room for God by loving Him the right way. If you want to be passionate for the rest of your life, keep drawing near to God for the rest of your life.

We must also make room for others. You're not on this journey alone. You were made to be in relationship and fellowship with others. Look at Ecclesiastics 4:9-10, "Two are better than one, because if one falls down his friend can help him up. But pity the man who falls down and has no one to help him up." We're not in this world by ourselves, therefore we need each other. Besides, what good will it do to make it all the way to the top and not have anyone to share it with. So make room for others, because you just never know when you may need them to encourage you, to cheer you, or to help you back up if you fall along the way.

Once you have discovered what truly inspires you and makes you feel alive, your passion will kick in and serve as the driving force, motivating you to complete your journey and reach your destiny. I really believe that passion is the key to your fulfillment and purpose in life. It is your passion that will cause you to think about, dream about, and get excited about who you are, where you're going, and what you will do in life. Passion is what makes life come alive, and the impossible possible. Apathy, indifference, low self-esteem, depression, emptiness, and lack of inspiration, will all fade away in the presence of your passion. Your passion will make your journey feel like something you want to do, and not something you have to do. And finally, your passion will become contagious, prompting others around you to become excited, supportive, and even passionate about your mission and goals in life.

I want to close this chapter with a beautiful poem I discovered. It really touched my heart, and I hope it touches yours as well.

BE PASSIONATE THROUGH LIFE!

Be passionate

When one is passionate there is a deep desire. A fire inside. And the will to approach life's circumstances and challenges, in a real way both to yourself and others. To explore your creative side, express yourself, in depth and knowledge. There is no need to be quiet. There is no need to hold back. Run free and explore your life. With perseverance, consistency,

Always listening

The inner ability to strive on, to proceed in power love and a sound mind. Be willing, be able to strive on with passion, but let wisdom be your guard, let understanding build character in you, appreciate beauty, sincerity, purity. Keep it close never exchange it. For it is like hidden treasure waiting to be discovered.

- Poetry of Life

Don't ever allow anything in life to kill your passion for life. Keep your head up, and the rest of you will stay up as well. I hear passion saying, "Okay, let's turn the page so we can move on."

CHAPTER EIGHT

FOLLOW PEACE

Peace: *Freedom from disturbance; quiet and tranquility.*

Years ago, I had a speaking engagement at a church about seventy miles from my home. I'd been to that church several times as a little boy, but that had been a long time ago. Several members of our church planned to drive down with me to lend their support. I distinctively remember hearing a small, still voice say to me on more than one occasion to call ahead for directions. I dismissed that voice each time because I was pretty sure that I could remember how to get to the church. After all, it was a small little church in a small little town. Well we all met up at the designated departure location. We left on time, with ten cars following the lead car, which happened to be my car. That's right, everybody was following me and after an hour and thirty two minutes everybody realized that we were lost. I had led parishioners, family, and friends astray. After going in circles and wasting a whole lot of time, someone in another car who was not filled with pride stopped and asked one of the locals for directions. A few minutes later, we were at the church, late but there. The lesson here is to be careful who you follow in life because they may not know where they're going either.

On the journey to our destination, one of the best pieces of advice that we could ever receive is to follow peace. Go where peace is going and you'll know that you're where you're supposed to be. We can have peace in a world filled with uncertainties. In life, we'll either have peace or we'll find ourselves going to pieces.

CHECK FOR PEACE

Someone should have checked to see if I knew where I was going on that warm Sunday afternoon before deciding to follow me. Seriously though, we must learn to follow the peace of God. If we listen to God and obey His every word we will have peace. It is His peace that assures us that we're on the right path, and headed in the right direction. When we don't have the peace of God, we find ourselves frustrated, confused, and feeling lost. One things for sure, the Lord will never lead us astray, and He will never cause us to become lost. So check for peace. If you don't have peace about a thing, that's usually a sign that it's not from God.

Peace says don't worry, don't stress out, don't get worked up, don't be afraid, don't let it get you down, and don't do something foolish.

Colossians 3:15 – Let the peace of Christ [the inner calm of one who walks daily with Him] be the controlling factor in your hearts [deciding and settling questions that arise]. To this peace indeed you were called as members in one body [of believers]. And be thankful [to God always]. - AMP

If you allow the Word of God along with the peace of God, that "inner calm" to dwell in your heart, every question or concern you have about life will be adequately answered by our Heavenly Father.

The definition of Peace is tranquility and a state of mental calm and serenity. The biblical definition of peace is "to be in right relationship with God." Think about it, when we're in right relationship with God, we have no worries at all, and this brings real peace.

John14:27 – Peace I leave with you; My own peace I now give and bequeath to you. Not as the world gives do I give to you. Do not let your hearts be troubled, neither let them be afraid. Stop allowing yourselves to be agitated and disturbed; and do not permit yourselves to be fearful and intimidated and cowardly and unsettled. AMP

Jesus came to offer us peace, His peace. Always look for the Lord's peace. It's easy to spot peace because it's always producing freedom from anxiety, worry, stress, disturbance, agitation, war, commotion, quarrels, fear, terror, anger, turmoil, chaos, drama, confusion, discord and anything else that is not like God.

PEACE BEGINS WITH GOD

God promises to give us peace and direction for every decision we have to make in life. So then, the first step in having real peace does not begin with people, places, money, or things; it begins with God. Real peace begins when we have peace with our Real God. To obtain good success in life, we must have peace with God and the peace of God. How do we obtain this? Well, there is only one way.

> *Ephesian 2:13-14 – But now in Christ Jesus,*
> *you who once were so far away, by the blood*
> *of Christ have been brought near. For He is*
> *our peace our bond of unity and harmony. -*
> *AMP*

The apostle Paul is saying that our sins had taken us far away from God. As a result, we had no promise, no hope and no peace. But God, the Father, sent His Son, Jesus, to reestablish that peace and hope. When we choose Jesus to be our Savior, He gives us peace with God. His peace clears the way, and then leads the way to the abundant life that He promised in His Word.

> *John 14:6 - Jesus saith unto him, I am the way, the truth, and the life: no man cometh unto the Father, but by me.*

Here, Jesus makes it clear that genuine and lasting peace begins with His Father and continues through Him. If we want to have peace in our homes, relationships, jobs, churches, communities, and peace in our hearts, we must first have peace with God and His Son, Jesus Christ.

> *John 16:33 - These things I have spoken unto you, that in me ye might have peace. In the world ye shall have tribulation: but be of good cheer; I have overcome the world.*

I believe that God wants us to live in peace. In fact that's one of the reasons He sent His Son to earth, so there would peace in the world, and peace in the hearts of man-kind. However, it seems like forever now, that world leaders, politicians, protestors, and even many religious leaders have failed to realize that the lack of peace is not because of the strife that is in the world, but rather the absence of peace in the human heart. As long as we live in this world, there will be a need for peace. Nice words, beautiful gifts, well thought out treaties, and love conferences are all good, but they don't produce real peace. Real peace comes from the Prince of

Peace and His name is Jesus. This is why it is so important for us to get to know, and follow the Prince of Peace.

PEACE WITHIN

The roads and highways we travel on seem to be filled with people who are in a big hurry to get somewhere, or in many cases nowhere. Many drivers become frustrated and hostile towards one another, often leading to road rage. Incidents of road rage are at an all-time high in our country. Road rage is a motorist's uncontrolled anger, and is usually provoked by another motorist's irritating act. It is expressed in aggressive or violent behavior.

I believe that individual inward peace would eliminate rage on the roadways, as well as the rage we often encounter in life. To make it far in life or anywhere at all, we must possess inward peace. No peace inside usually means no peace outside. God has put His Spirit as well as His Kingdom on the inside of us.

The Pharisees wanted to know from Jesus, when the Kingdom of God would come. The Lord told them that the Kingdom of God is not here or there, but that the Kingdom of God is within us, in our hearts and surrounding us. What do we get when the Kingdom of God comes in us?

Romans 14:17 – For the Kingdom of God is
not a matter of what we eat or drink, but of

living a life of goodness and peace and joy in
the Holy Spirit. - NLT

Everything we need for the good life and peace is already in us. So, there is no need for us to go looking anywhere else for what we already have.

You may lose your job, your family, and all of your friends. You may no longer be popular or feel accepted.

The doctor may give you a bad report, and your world may be falling apart. But you can remain quiet, calm, and under control because of the peace of God that is within you. Godly peace is internal and not external. No matter what happens on the outside we can remain calm because Christ has given us peace on the inside. What happens when we're not in peace? We worry, get upset, become afraid, become irritable, yell, lash out, want to fight, and we turn to the world. But remember, wherever Jesus is, there will always be the presence of His peace. His peace keeps us from giving in and giving up. His peace keeps us on the right road and with the right attitude. His peace reminds us that God is still in control of us, and everything around us. Finally, look at what happens to people who have peace within.

Proverbs 14:30 – "A peaceful heart leads to
a healthy body" – NLT

Do you see that? Peace is something that the doctor could literally prescribe for what ails most us. Peace takes away sadness and sorrow and eliminates stress, anxiety, fear and worry. Believe it or not, many of these things are what make us sick on the journey of life.

But when peace is reigning in our hearts, we feel better in our bodies and in our minds. We feel better about who we are and where we're going in life.

PEACE WITH OTHERS

Your purpose in life will never just be about you. It will always include, involve, and have an impact on others. Therefore, the Bible tells us to make every effort to live in peace with other people.

> *Romans 12:18 – If it be possible, as much as lieth in you, live peaceably with all men.*

We are required to do everything in our power to be peaceful with all people. Remember, we cannot live in peace with one another unless we have the peace of God operating within us. We should always strive for peace because peace makes the road less bumpy and the trip more enjoyable. Look at the honor that Jesus bestows upon those who seek after peace:

> *Matthew 5:9 – Blessed are the peacemakers: for they shall be called the children of God.*

People who go after peace are called blessed and happy.

The peace within us blesses us and blesses those who are around us as well. The peace we possess can bring together family members, friends, nations, and even enemies. God is always glorified when we bring peace to where there is none. When we bring peace to a situation, what we're doing is pointing people to the answer and the answer is always Jesus. That too, is part of our purpose. The Lord commands us to be people of peace. He empowers us to be people who are proactive, intentional, and people who go way out of their way to do the things that make for peace.

We also have to stay away from things and people that continue to cause division and strife, thus breaking the peace. Look at the strong words used in this next passage:

> *2 Timothy 2:23-24 – But refuse (shut your mind against, have nothing to do with) trifling (ill-informed, unedifying, stupid) controversies over ignorant questionings, for you know that they foster strife and breed quarrels. And the servant of the Lord must not be quarrelsome (fighting and contending).*

*Instead, he must be kindly to everyone and
mild-tempered preserving the bond of peace;
he must be a skilled and suitable teacher, pa-
tient and forbearing and willing to suffer
wrong. - AMPC*

We have been called to preserve the peace and not participate in breaking it. The spirit of peace must always abound
in us. The truth is, there is no peace inside, outside of Jesus
Christ. In other words, there can be no peace around us, if
the Lord's peace is not found in us. Peace for the believer
must become a real priority.

PEACE – REVIEW AND REWIND

Why the review and rewind? Because peace plays a major
role in you having a successful journey. Why? Because the
absence of peace can cause you to miss out on, and never
reach your full potential in life. If you want to have the peace
of God, review these facts and don't forget them.

1. We may as well face it; we will never be able to find
    lasting and genuine peace in anything that comes
    from this world. Why? Because all of the things of
    this world eventually fade away. Real peace does not
    come from a career, title, position, house, automo-
    bile, prestige, status, money, or possessions. There's
    absolutely nothing wrong with any of these, but none
    of these things can produce peace alone. In fact, it's

very possible to have all of those things and still not have real peace. That's because true peace comes only from Jesus, the Prince of Peace.

2. Jesus told us and showed us in the Scriptures, everything we needed to know about having and maintain peace.

3. Psalm 119:165 – "Great peace have they which love thy law." All we need to know about peace is in the Word of God. Philippians 4:7 - And the peace of God, which passeth all understanding, shall keep your hearts and minds through Christ Jesus. The peace of God is designed to keep us. It's given to us to keep us up, to keep us standing, to keep us strong, and to keep us trusting.

4. This peace of God also keeps us going, and loving, and forgiving, and hoping, and believing, and singing, and shouting and waiting for Christ's return.

5. Being a peacemaker is necessary if we're going to get along with others. When our words, thoughts and actions are peaceful, we know that we're on the right track. Matthew 5:9 - You're blessed when you can show people how to cooperate instead of compete or fight. That's when you discover who you really are and your place in God's family. - MSG

Thank God for His peace! Get right up on the bumper of peace, and follow as close as you can. Don't worry, you won't be ticketed for following too closely. Wherever the peace of God goes, make sure that's where you're going as well.

CHAPTER NINE

DON'T STOP

Stop: *To discontinue or cease from movement.*

I remember when my dad was teaching me how to drive. He was terrified to say the least. As we both sat there in the car, his first word of instruction to me was - don't. Don't take your eyes off the road. Don't make a turn without signaling first. Don't turn on the radio. Don't ride in both lanes. Don't drive too fast. Don't drive too slowly. Don't slam on the breaks. Don't drive too close to the vehicle in front of you. Don't be looking around and don't be nervous. When he finished with all of his don'ts, I asked him if it was okay for me to put the key in the ignition and start the car so we could leave, and he said, "Don't be funny."

There are some don'ts that I would like to share with you when it comes to your purpose and destiny in life. If you're like me, there have probably been plenty of times when you felt like giving up. In fact, you may feel like quitting and throwing in the towel right now. But I beg you, please don't.

DON'T STOP. Don't give up now. You see if you keep stopping and starting and stopping and starting you'll never get to where you're supposed to be. We've been called to persevere. Perseverance is being steadfast in doing something despite the difficulty or delay in achieving success. Your goals are reachable and attainable. So as you close in on reaching your dreams, make sure you remember these important don'ts.

DON'T BE AFRAID

We don't have to be afraid to travel the pathways of life because God travels with us. The Lord gives us the power to successfully conquer and overcome every fear that would hold us back. Fear comes from the devil.

His plan and purpose is to use fear to stop us and leave us right where we are. Please understand and realize that God opposes fear. It is not God's will for us to walk around afraid and in fear. Fear brings us down by destroying the relationship and fellowship we have with our Heavenly Father. Therefore, fear cannot be of God or come from God.

> *II Timothy 1:7 – For God hath not given us the spirit of fear; but of power, and of love, and of a sound mind.*

Now take a look at this same verse from the Amplified version of the Bible. It further proves and exposes the truth about fear.

104

6

> *II Timothy 1:7 – For God did not give us a spirit of timidity (of cowardice, of craven and cringing and fawning fear), but He has given us a spirit of power and of love and of calm and well-balanced mind and discipline and self-control. -AMP*

So there you have it, God does not give us a spirit or attitude of fear. But what He does give us is everything we need to overcome fear. The grip of fear can cause some serious issues in our lives. Take a look at this incomplete list of problems that can stem from the emotion of fear. This is what fear can do to us if we allow it into our lives.

1. Fear immobilizes us.
2. Fear leads to sin.
3. Fear causes physical problems.
4. Fear brings confusion.
5. Fear causes us to hide.
6. Fear causes us to abandon our love for others.
7. Fear keeps us from serving God.
8. Fear causes us to flee when we should be standing.
9. Fear keeps us from dreaming and setting goals.
10. Fear keeps us from believing.
11. Fear opens the door to sudden destruction.

In fact the Bible teaches us that fear is a trap, and anything that is trapped cannot proceed, progress, produce, or move forward.

> *Proverbs 25:29 – Fearing people is a dangerous trap, but trusting the Lord means safety. - NLT*

I believe that fear played a major role in the catastrophic events that exploded into Job's life. I could never understand why the Lord would allow such horrific events of adversity to come upon Job and his family. The Bible said that Job was a righteous man. Job was a man who loved God and abstained from evil.

I was in that group that believed that somehow God was trying to teach Job a valuable lesson. Or maybe God allowed all of these things to happen to Job so that He could show up on the scene and fix them. But then in my reading and study time I stumbled across Job 3:25 and the light came on.

> *Job 3:25 – For the thing which I greatly feared is come upon me, and that which I was afraid of is come unto me.*

There it is. Even when everything was going well, Job feared that something bad was going to happen. Job confessed that he greatly feared that these things would come on him. He erected and then opened the door of fear, and the devil walked right in and wreaked havoc in his life.

Satan does not always use guns or knives to bring fear upon us. He also uses our past sins, the uncertainty of the future, the potential of failure, and the possibility of criticism to keep us from moving forward. But thanks be to God we don't have to be afraid. We don't have to live in fear another second because God has given us everything we need to overcome fear.

You may be thinking, what if fear comes anyway. Well I suggest you do what King David did.

> *Psalm 56:3 – But when I am afraid, I will put*
> *my trust in you. - NLT*

When fear drives into your life, trust God even more. Putting our trust in God causes our fears to make a U-turn. The Lord will send them right back from whence they came – and that's from the devil, and the pit of hell.

DON'T BE DISCOURAGED

Discouragement is a loss of confidence or enthusiasm or a feeling of rejection, hopelessness, and despair. There are many things that can cause us to become discouraged to the point that we want to give up on our dreams.

The loss of a loved one, the loss of a job, medical conditions, lack of finances, lack of support, broken promises, broken relationships, all can serve as tools of discouragement. The good news is we can overcome discouragement and the things that cause us to become discouraged in the first place. We have to decide that we will not live in the miserable pit of discouragement. Instead we must look to what is shared in God's Word concerning how to deal with this foe.

> *Psalm 42:5- NLT – Why am I discouraged? Why is my heart so sad? I will put my hope in God! I will praise him again, my Savior and my God!*

In the midst of struggles and adversity the psalmist would ask himself two questions and would follow those two questions with two bold statements. Putting our hope in God and praising God is the cure for discouragement. Where does discouragement really come from? It comes from Satan, of course.

We must exert our will, power and authority over the enemy and what he is trying to do to us through the spirit of discouragement. It can become so easy for us to succumb to the tricky trap of discouragement. When you feel discouragement coming on, don't stick around, quickly get out of its way. The cure for discouragement is to move deeper into the presence of God. As we draw closer to Him, and truly surrender ourselves to Him, something amazing happens.

James 4:7 – Submit yourselves therefore to God. Resist the devil, and he will flee from you.

Do you see what happens? Satan leaves us, and he takes the spirit of discouragement with him. We were not created to be sad and depressed; we're not creatures of doom and gloom. We must be positive, looking for the good and not the bad. The way we overcome the devil and his tactics of discouragement is by giving ourselves totally to the Lord. Truly submitting our lives to God gives us the power to resist Satan, causing him to leave us alone.

DON'T LOOK BACK

Why should we not look back? Because God has something that's so much better in front of us. As Christians, we can't move forward in faith if we're constantly looking behind us in the rearview mirror of the past. Yesterday is gone and there is nothing we can do about it. We cannot change the past but we can help determine our future. If we want to gain momentum for the good things that are to come, we must stop dragging our past behind us and let it go.

My grandfather was a farmer; he just loved growing things. I remember him plowing in his garden sometimes with an old red tiller. I noticed he never looked back. His eyes were always pointed in the direction he wanted to go. The point is a farmer can't plow a straight line if he or she is looking backwards. So don't look back!

> *Luke 9:62 – And Jesus said unto him, "No man, having put his hand to the plough, and looking back, is fit for the kingdom of God."*

Jesus said that looking back makes a person unfit for God's Kingdom. When we continuously look back at our past, it literally makes us useless for the future. Holding onto yesterday keeps us from discovering our today, and even our tomorrows. Looking back causes us to be out of place, and looking back could also cause us to go back. Your purpose and God's plan is in front of you, so you must look ahead.

> *Philippians 3:13 – "No, dear brothers and sisters, I have not achieved it, but I focus on this one thing: Forgetting the past and looking forward to what lies ahead" – NLT*

Everything that we will ever be or accomplish in life is in front of us and not behind us. Often times the past wants to show up in the present so that present can become trapped by the past. Holding on to past sins, past crimes, past failures, past broken hearts, past relationships, past broken promises, and even past successes will only keep you from reaching opportunities and blessings in the future. Everything about the past is over and your future awaits you. You can look at the past to learn from it, and that's all. Living in the past is a "destiny killer" therefore it is prohibited, and not allowed under any circumstances.

> *Isaiah 43:18 – Remember ye not the former*
> *things, neither consider the things of old.*

God is encouraging us to forget about the past and close the door on it. Guess what? The past has passed, it's over, it's gone, and there is nothing that can ever change it. God is much more interested in your future than He is your past. He is more interested in where you're going than where you've been. So get up and turn away from the dark days of yesterday and what could have been and what should have been, and look unto Jesus the author and finisher of your faith.

DON'T STOP BELIEVING

Do you believe in miracles? Do you believe in your dreams? Do you believe that God has big plans for your life? I hope and pray that you answered yes to all three of these questions. Sometimes the difference between success and failure comes down to what we believe. Look at what Jesus said about believing.

> *Mark 9:23 – Jesus said unto him, If thou*
> *canst believe, all things are possible to him*
> *that believeth.*

Your purpose, destiny, and God-given dreams will continue to live as long as you believe and stand on His promises. Notice the Lord said all things are possible based on what we believe, not what we can do. What should we believe? We should always believe what God has promised and said to us in His Word. Hearing the Word of God produces the faith we need to believe.

In the book of Numbers in the Old Testament, God promised to give the land of Canaan to the children of Israel. Moses sent twelve men to search out this land. When this group of spies returned there were two different stories and reactions to what they had seen. Ten of the men gave a report of doom, gloom, and impossibilities. But Joshua and Caleb's account was quite different. They believed that they could take the land that the Lord promised they could have.

> *Numbers 13:30-31 – 30 And Caleb stilled the people before Moses, and said, Let us go up at once, and possess it; for we are well able to overcome it. 31 But the men that went up with him said, We be not able to go up against the people; for they are stronger than we.*

The reason Caleb and Joshua were so upbeat and positive was because they believed that God would be faithful to His Word. You have to be the same way. You must keep believing God's promises no matter how bad things may appear to be. Remember God cannot lie. So instead of focusing on the situation, or the negative circumstances, or the obstacles that may be in your way, focus on God. When the unpleasant facts are staring you directly in your face, believe that God will change those facts because of your faith. There is nothing too hard or too difficult for God. Nothing!

DON'T GIVE UP

Sometimes getting there will not be easy at all. Can I get a witness? Sometimes we may feel like giving up because "there" seems so far away, and sometimes "there" seems to elude us altogether. But please, please don't quit now. My grandmother use to say, "The darkest hour is just before day." That's so true, because sometimes our destiny, our breakthrough, and our finest hour is just inches in front of us. Getting that college degree, starting a business, becoming a missionary, or realizing your dream may be much closer than you think. So now is not the time to quit. Not now, and not ever.

> *Galatians 6:9 says, Let us not become weary*
> *in doing good, for at the proper time we will*
> *reap a harvest if we do not give up.*

The road to our destiny and fulfilled dreams will always come with challenges along the way. But those challenges and adverse circumstances are nothing more than speed bumps. Speed bumps are never meant to stop us, they are only there just to slow us down. I believe that some speed bumps are strategically place in our lives by God. Why? Because sometimes we're moving too fast. Sometimes they're placed in our lives to slow us down enough so that we will avoid what would have been an accident just up the road. Still other speed bumps are there to slow us down so we can see, and appreciate our journey as we travel. Sometimes we can become so focused on our destiny, that we never take the time to really enjoy the journey that will get us there.

Satan also places speed bumps along our way. His purpose is always to hinder us and to stop us. But please remember this, Satan may slow us down from time to time, but he can never stop us. This is especially true when we go after the Lord with our whole heart. Seeking the Kingdom of God must become our top priority in life. When we put God first we come to realize that it really does not matter what the devil is doing or trying to do in our lives. Putting God first keeps us on track, His blessing before us, and it keeps Satan just where he should be, behind us, in our rearview mirror.

> *Matthew 6:33 – But first and most importantly seek (aim at, strive after) His kingdom and His righteousness [His way of doing and being right—the attitude and character of God], and all these things will be given to you also. - AMP*

> *Psalm 37:4 says, "Delight thyself also in the Lord: and he shall give thee the desires of thine heart."*

God is really interested in giving us the desires of our hearts. We need to make certain that our desires line up with His will and His Word. The things you desire may not come as fast as you would like them to, but remember the Lord will always show up and give you the motivation and inspiration you need to keep you pressing on. Success will come and your dreams will be discovered in God's time. But in the meantime you remain faithful to the Lord.

Waiting on God is never a waste of time. Serving, and believing in the Lord will pay off after a while. So don't give up, and don't stop now. You are closer to your destiny than you've ever been in your life. You've invested a lot of sweat, tears, pain, and hope. You've come a mighty long way, so quitting for you is not an option, not now, not ever. Keep the faith and stay the course, and don't stop.

CHAPTER TEN

ARRIVE AT YOUR DESTINATION

***Arrive:** To reach a destination.*

I always love to hear Wilma say those four wonderful words, "arriving at your destination." Oh, excuse my manners. Wilma is the name my wife and I assigned to the voice of the GPS on our phones. She knows exactly where we are at all times. She tells us which route to take and how long it will take to get to where we're going. She tells us when to turn, when to merge, and even when there are traffic delays. And when we fail to listen to Wilma or follow her instructions perfectly, she admonishes us with phrases like rerouting, recalculating, or make a U-turn when possible. Eventually, she leads us to the place we told her we wanted to go. Wilma is very smart, but she's nowhere near as smart as our God. And truth be told, she's led us astray on more than one occasion.

Another truth is God never leads us astray. He never leads us to the wrong place, and He never leads us to a dead-end.

If we listen to Him and follow His instructions we will arrive at our divine destination. God is our Supernatural GPS in life and for life.

How wonderful will it be to hear your Heavenly Father declare, "You Have Arrived at Your Destination." Maybe it will be that dream job, or graduating from college. Maybe it will be starting your own business, or marrying your spouse and starting a family. Maybe it will be rescuing a loved one from an addictive behavior, or writing a book. Maybe it will be getting physically fit, or building a home from the ground up, or simply retiring and enjoying your golden years. Whatever the case, believe in your heart that you will arrive, and believe that God has provided everything you need to get there.

YOU MADE IT

I remember the first and only time my family drove from Tuscaloosa, Alabama to Los Angeles California. What a road trip! Two thousand twenty eight miles was the distance between our house and Aunt Doris' house out on the west coast. Two thousand twenty eight miles of driving, and driving, and more driving. Two thousand twenty eight miles of summer heat, deserts, pop-up storms. Two thousand twenty eight miles of pit stops, bathroom breaks, and filling up. Two thousand twenty eight miles of being cooped up in a grey Cadillac Deville where the radio stopped working and the air conditioner would soon follow. Two thousand twenty eight miles of crankiness, frustration, and getting on each other's nerves. It looked like we would never make it, but we did. After two and a half days we saw that sign that said Los Angeles City Limit. After all of that time, we'd finally made it. Finally making it is what makes the journey worth it.

Praise God, you made it! That's right, you made it! "You made it," implies accomplishment and achievement. Just like we made that trip by pressing on, even when circumstances made the journey unpleasant, you too, can make it in the face of any kind of adversity. You can make it in the midst of overwhelming odds. You can make it although the journey may be long and tedious. You may have doubts, confusion, rough roads, haters, stumbling blocks, setbacks, traps, and wrong turns along the way, but you can make it. You can make it even when you think you can't and others swear you won't. You can reach your goal, and you can discover your purpose and God's plan for your life. You can make it but you can't make it alone. Remember God is there with you, leading you, guiding you, and helping you every step of the way.

> *Philippians 1:6 – "Being confident of this very thing, that he which hath begun a good work in you will perform it until the day of Jesus Christ."*

Don't forget it was God who started you on this journey to your destiny, and He always finishes what He starts. He ordered and ordained your great purpose for life before you even became a life.

This is why we put our hope and trust in Him, the One who is constant, consistent, and never changing. He never relents, and He never gives up on us. God is always working in us and working for us. He is why we make it, and He is the reason we succeed in life.

> *Ephesians 2:10 – For we are his workman-ship, created in Christ Jesus unto good works, which God hath before ordained that we should walk in them.*

> *Ephesians 2:10 - For we are His workman-ship [His own master work, a work of art],* created *in Christ Jesus [reborn from above—spiritually transformed, renewed, ready to be used] for good works, which God prepared [for us] beforehand [taking paths which He set], so that we would walk in them [living the good life which He prearranged and made ready for us]. – AMP*

These are shouting words, and exciting news! The God of this universe made you on purpose for a purpose. This is why it was so important to your Heavenly Father that you make it. God was, is, and always will be your biggest fan.

You can make it, but you must not give in to your doubters, your enemies, or even yourself. You can make it if you do not quit when everything inside of you wants to throw in the towel. The Bible says, "The race is not given to the swift, nor the battle to the strong." The reward goes to those who are willing to endure to the very end. Anyone can start a race, but it takes grit, perseverance, and determination to finish the race. You can become part of a very special club. You can be divinely and officially inducted into what I call the Hall of Fame of Finishers.

You may be saying, "But pastor, how can this be? I haven't even really gotten started yet." I know you haven't, but by faith you will start, and by faith you will finish!

THIS IS WHY YOU WERE BORN

Mark Twain once said, "There are two great days in our lives, the day we are born and the day we discover why we were born." Your purpose in life is why you were born. No one can do what God has called you to do, and no one can be what God has created you to be. When you discover your purpose and His plan for your life, your existence will take on true meaning and fulfillment.

Jeremiah *1:5* – *"Before I formed thee in the belly I knew thee; and before thou camest forth out of the womb I sanctified thee, and I ordained thee a prophet unto the nations."*

Psalm 139:13-19 – "For thou hast possessed my reins: thou hast covered me in my mother's womb. I will praise thee; for I am fearfully and wonderfully made: marvellous are thy works; and that my soul knoweth right well. My substance was not hid from thee, when I was made in secret, and curiously wrought in the lowest parts of the earth. Thine eyes did see my substance, yet being unperfect; and in thy book all my members were written, which in continuance were fashioned, when as yet there was none of them. How precious also are thy thoughts unto me, O God! How great is the sum of them!"

The God of this universe knows exactly why He brought you into this world. He knew that He had great plans for you all along. You were always a thought in His mind even before you came to be. You were created and crafted by the hands of the Divine, and that makes your purpose divine. So it's really true, you were born for this.

Queen Esther was born to break her silence and save her people from being exterminated by an evil man who had an evil plan. Moses was born to lead the Children of Israel from under the bondage of Pharaoh all the way to the Promise Land. Noah was born to build the ark in order to preserve his family and the human race from the flood when the rains finally came. John the Baptist was born to be the forerunner of Jesus Christ, paving the way for the Savior of the world. Paul was born to preach the gospel to Jews and Gentiles, and to write most of the New Testament that is still being read to this very day. And then there was Jesus! Jesus was born to be an example to all, to die for the sins of all, and to offer up salvation and eternal life to the whole world through His death, burial, and resurrection. And you were born to fulfil your purpose and His plan for your life, and by His grace you will! Yes, you will! Go ahead and say it. Say, YES I WILL!

ALL THINGS WORK TOGETHER

It may not have seemed like it at the time but perhaps now you can see how all things, good and bad, have worked out for your greater good! Sometimes God takes the worst thing that ever happened to us in life, and causes it to work out to be the best thing that ever happened to us in life.

Remember God always has a purpose for everything that occurs in our lives – the ups and downs, the successes and failures, the births and the deaths, the trials and tribulations, the good times and the bad times, and the joys and sorrows. One of the basic biblical truths about every child of God, is nothing comes into our lives without our heavenly Father's knowledge and permission.

> *Romans 8:28 – "We know that in all things God works for the good of those who love him, who have been called according to his purpose." – NIV*

Your journey has not been just a series of random happenings, occurrences, circumstances, and events. Everything that God did or allowed in your life was intentional. Please understand I'm not saying that God orchestrates the problems that show up in our lives. In fact, I'm convinced that most of the negative things that happen to us, are of our own doing.

Bad things usually happen because of the bad decisions and choices we made, or the bad decisions and choices that others around us made. But even then, God had our purpose in mind. So no matter what happens or what circumstances we may face in life; God can and will bring something good out of it.

God does not just use our good experiences in life; He also uses the bad experiences, the ugly experiences, and the secret experiences in our lives to carve out a beautiful future for us when we dare to trust Him. God can take all of our little messes and make one big miracle out of them. All things working together means our final outcome will be for our good and God's glory.

REROUTING

Your final destination is not in this world, but it is literally out of this world. Your ultimate goal is to one day be with your Father and His Son Jesus Christ in Heaven. Contrary to what many people believe, heaven is a real place. After our work and purpose on earth are done, we are dispatched to a place called heaven, which is the presence of God. Heaven is the believer's eternal home of everlasting redemption, re-generation, and peace.

> Philippians *3:20 – "But our citizenship is in heaven, from which also we eagerly wait for a Savior, the Lord Jesus Christ."*

Jesus made it very clear that heaven is a very real place. Heaven is a prepared place for a prepared people. Jesus said, "In my Father's house are many mansions: if it were not so, I would have told you. I go to prepare a place for you. And if I go and prepare a place for you, I will come again, and receive you unto myself; that where I am, there ye may be also." Nothing on earth can compete with or be compared to heaven. It is a place of inconceivable blessing, and its value was worth Christ dying for. The Bible teaches us that only those who have been redeemed by the blood of Jesus Christ will be able to enter there.

Revelation 21:4 – "And God shall wipe away all tears from their eyes; and there shall be no more death, neither sorrow, nor crying, neither shall there be any more pain: for the former things are passed away."

In heaven everything is new and regenerated. The heavens and earth are regenerated. This exciting new place the Lord has created for us is free from sin, sorrow, sickness, suffering, and separation. We will never die again because death will be dead forever. There will be no tears in heaven for you and me. The Bible says, "No eye has seen, no ear has heard, no mind has conceived what God has prepared for those who love him."

One day the Lord Himself will reroute your life and the direction of your existence from earth to heaven, and this will be your final destination. Heaven will be the last stop on your amazing journey. Yes, heaven is your purpose and His ultimate plan for your life. Praise God!

Prayer For Salvation

Say this prayer out loud right now to receive Jesus Christ as your Lord and personal Savior.

"Dear God, I want to be a part of your family. I acknowledge that Jesus died for my sins and that You raised Jesus from the dead, and I now accept Him as my Lord and personal Savior. I accept my salvation from sin right now. I am now saved. Thank you, Father God, for forgiving me, saving me, and giving me eternal life with You, through your Son Jesus Christ. Amen!"

Welcome to the Family of God!

Congratulations! You are now a part of the precious Family of God! I would love to pray for you and provide you with resources to help you in your new walk with God.

Please contact me at

pastorcherry@hightown.org
or
info@marvincherry.com

About The Author

Pastor Cherry has been chosen and called by Almighty God to preach the Gospel of Jesus Christ. He is an anointed, gifted Bible teacher and preacher, and has served as the Senior Pastor of Hightown Church of God for over two decades.

Pastor Cherry is married to his loving wife Candace, and has three sons, Christopher, Caleb, and Micah, and a granddaughter, Prezleigh. His greatest passion in life is to preach and teach the Gospel of the love and grace of God that comes through a relationship with His Son Jesus Christ. His hope is that people from all walks of life will exchange ordinary living for extraordinary life through the transforming power of Jesus Christ.